Profiles from the Past

Profiles from the Past

An Uncommon History of Vermont

CORA CHENEY

The Countryman Press

TAFTSVILLE, VERMONT

Library of Congress Cataloging in Publication Data

Cheney, Cora.
  Profiles from the past.

  "First published as weekly newspaper columns in the
Brattleboro reformer, the Bennington banner, and the
Burlington free press."
  Includes index.
  1. Vermont — History — Collected works. I. Title.
F49.C5   974.3″008   76-28335
ISBN 0-914378-15-5

Printed in the United States of America
by the Whitman Press, Lebanon, New Hampshire

CONTENTS

Foreword

SECTS, ANTI-SLAVERY, & MIGRATIONS

SUFFRAGE, DEPRESSION, & CONSERVATION

Foreword

This is an "uncommon history of Vermont," as the title says. It starts with Indians and ends with Act 250, and in between is a fascinating, people-oriented history of Vermont. Most readers probably didn't know, for example, that Samuel de Champlain didn't follow the general custom of the time of seducing Indian girls. People also may have overlooked the fact that John Conant of Brandon made the first cast iron stoves in Vermont, thereby liberating housewives of his era from the tyranny of slaving over a hot fireplace all day.

Champlain's alleged virtue (he later married a 12-year-old Parisian girl) and Conant's stoves have one thing in common: they are facts plucked by Cora Cheney in her search to make the history of her adopted state come vividly to life.

This is an "uncommon" history, too, because it is a series of profiles—profiles of Vermont's past. They are short episodes because they originally were written as weekly newspaper columns. Their advantage as newspaper columns was that, over a period of two years, they treated readers of the Brattleboro *Reformer*, the Bennington *Banner* and the Burlington *Free Press* to quick glimpses into yesteryears. The disadvantage is that over a period of seven days, from the appearance of one column to the next, readers tended to lose continuity. That's why it is delightful that the columns now have been collected in book form.

Cora Cheney is fascinated with people. She originally wrote for us at *The Reformer* a series of "profiles" of Vermonters, from town clerks to politicians. When that series was finished she hit upon the idea of continuing the "profile" technique, but this time profiling facets of Vermont history rather than individuals.

When Cora tackles something, she does it with enthusiasm. As this is being written in the summer of 1976, for example, Cora, her husband Benjamin, and her two college-age children, Mary and Alan, are hiking in the Arctic. No doubt we will be treated someday to profiles of polar bears. That would be typical. Cora uses life as her resource book.

Born in Alabama, she studied journalism at the University of Georgia, acquiring in both locations a rich southern accent which says "Ei-yuh" with a drawl, a fascination with the written word, and Benjamin W. Partridge Jr. Ben is a Navy man, and after almost single-handedly defeating the Japanese at sea in World War II (or something like that), he, Cora and the children were assigned to many Navy posts around the world. They lived in Iceland, where they found a dog, the late Ensign, and in Taiwan, where Cora learned how to cook Chinese food to such perfection that it makes me hungry just to write this sentence. Meanwhile the wandering Partridges sought roots, and years ago they came to Vermont and bought an old farmhouse in South Windham, which you can't get to from here.

After retiring from the Navy, and traveling around the world, and camping in Africa where a rogue elephant ripped their tent apart one night because Ben poured pepper into its snout, the Partridges settled in Vermont. Cora continued to write children's books (she's published about 19 of them) and Ben set out to make Vermont safe from shabby land developers. Former Governor Deane C. Davis, whose foresight and wisdom enabled Vermont to become a world leader in environmental protection by his support for Act 250 and other legislation, named Ben Partridge chairman of the state Environmental Board and director of the State Planning Office.

As far as this book is concerned, these facts are important because, gentle reader, you will understand why Cora feels so strongly about the beauty of Vermont that she concludes her history with a chapter on Act 250. It's also important, because living part-time in Montpelier while her husband toiled there put Cora within a few minutes walk of the vast resources of the Vermont Historical Society, of which she is a trustee. Turn a professional journalist loose upon historic archives and you come up with "Profiles of the Past: An Uncommon History of Vermont."

Vermonters are a proud lot, particularly where their history is concerned. Often Cora's newspaper articles led Vermonters to send her anecdotes which led to further research and newer "profiles." She also found that Vermonters are touchy about particulars. If she said something happened at 4:35 p.m., she found out that it better not have happened at 4:33 p.m. And her research was so thorough that she was seldom, if ever, proved wrong.

An "uncommon history?" It's a good title for a book about a most uncommon, and wonderful, state.

—Norman Runnion

DEDICATION

To Ben, who endured me through 130 column deadlines and who listened to Vermont history beyond the call of duty — with love.

Wilderness, Wars & Statehood

1. The Indians

It all began with the Indians. Old records and history books as well as an abundance of relics found throughout Vermont tell us that Indians were here, three separate civilizations of them; they were numerous, an estimated 123,000 in 1616, in what is now Vermont, and they were active in making arrowheads and fighting each other and scalping white men, who, some people think, had it coming to them.

Authorities at the University of Vermont state that there are over 200 known Indian sites in Vermont, mostly on waterways. The Champlain Valley is probably the best known and best investigated of the Indian grounds, but the Connecticut, the Winooski, the Missisquoi, the West, and other stream banks have yielded a rich harvest of information and remains for the few archaeologists who have worked in this field.

One of the best known digs is at Swanton, with other excavated sites found at Orwell and at Groton where Lyndon State College has conducted research.

Indian culture began in Vermont with the so called *Paleo* Indians who lived so far in the prehistoric past that the ice cap was current news for them. Implements found in the Champlain Valley lead archaeologists to believe that they lived here from 9,000-10,000 years ago until 5000-2000 BC. It is probable that the sea came inland as far as Lake Champlain then and that the land was tundra, similar to that in Newfoundland. There were herd animals in plenty, and the living was easy. These Indians were related to, or at least influenced by, the Eskimos. They made their weapons of slate in Eskimo style. Various authorities refer to them as Eskimoid or Laurentian or Red Paint people because their graves contain red ocher, symbol of life. Hubbardton, Swanton, Orwell, and Otter Creek have evidence of these people.

This culture was replaced by the *Archaic* or *Pre-Algonquin* Indian group somewhere in the 5000-2000 BC period. Perhaps the change in the land, with coniferous trees beginning to take over the tundra, contributed to the change in people. The Archaic Indians hunted and fished and gathered food in the increasing broad-leafed forests. They did not have bows and arrows, which seem to have come later from other cultures. They hurled spears instead. Some of the tools used by the Archaic Indians were gouges, mortars and pestles, plummets, and spear heads.

It has been suggested that the gouges, which are rare in North American collections but found relatively often in Vermont, could have been maple taps. It would have been an easy matter to catch the sap in skin or bark buckets, but how did they boil it? Indian expert Tom Daniels says they boiled sap in clay pots, but no very large clay pots have been found and they are notoriously fragile on a fire; others think it possible that they used their usual boiling method of heating a stream rock and dropping it into a liquid-filled bark or hide container; Professor William Haviland of the University of Vermont doubts that they made syrup at all.

The third, and historic, group of Indians are the *Woodland* group, which includes the Iroquois and Algonquins who clashed with the European colonists. The Abnaki Tribe of the Algonquin nation were Vermont's best known Indians. The Iroquois had long hunted and camped on Lake Champlain shores, and when Samuel de Champlain arrived in 1609 on what was then called the Lake of the Iroquois, his first act was to shoot three of them. But at about that time the Abnakis retook this territory and were Vermont's chief foes in colonial Indian warfare. The Iroquois allied themselves with the English in New York State and the Abnakis with the French from Canada as lines were drawn for the French and Indian Wars, an unparalleled near-century of carnage.

A famous collection of Indian relics assembled by the late Leslie B. Truax of St. Albans was presented to the Fleming Museum at UVM some years ago. This collection contains some 25 different kinds of artifacts, including celts, pipes, pendants, gouges, tubes, axes, drills, mortars and pestles, arrow points, and scrapers.

Two rare types of relics found in Vermont are discoidals, circular shaped stones with two concave sides, probably used for a game; and banner stones, variously shaped stones with one or two holes drilled in them, which were apparently used by Archaic Indians as balances for spears thrown in hunting.

Indians made pottery in historic and prehistoric times, and an abundance of pottery shards found in old kitchen middens shows a variety of designs. Indians cooked meat on open hearth fires, but they also made stone-lined fire pits in which they heated rocks that were in turn dropped into birchbark, skin or pottery containers of liquid to boil water or cook stews. These old hearths and pits can be found near stream banks by alert campers or relic hunters. Roving Indians lived in caves and on streamside campsites or rock shelters were made with protecting skin walls. Prior to 1950 the State of Vermont provided a travelling exhibit of Indian relics that was shown to schools, but this was discontinued. Today many Vermonters are not aware of their rich archaeological heritage.

People who locate Indian relics are often astonished to find artifacts made from material that is not native to the region; archaeological sites in Vermont have yielded copper implements but there was no substantial copper deposit this side of Lake Superior. The fact is, the Indians travelled. The Vermont Indians summered where the berries were good and even planted crops of corn, beans and squash. They followed salmon streams where the fishing was good, and sometimes they went south, perhaps just for the fun of it. Of course they traded implements on their travels.

They had first-class travel facilities in the Vermont waterways. Lake Champlain offered excellent routes to those handy at making canoes. A favorite trip, and one still taken by canoe fans today, was to go up (south) Lake Champlain to Otter Creek and to its end; then a short portage over to the site of the present town of Weston taking the West River to the confluence of the Connecticut and thence south.

Another route which took one into Iroquois territory was to take Lake Champlain to its southern end and thence a portage to the Hudson and on south to Albany and below; or along the Winooski past Montpelier to the Connecticut Valley.

These streams, along with the many other rivers, brooks, and creeks that crisscross Vermont, offer fertile fields for relic hunters. The Connecticut River contains two celebrated stones covered with Indian pictograph writing, one at Bellows Falls and one at Brattleboro, the latter being under water since the building of the dam at Vernon.

There are remains of camps on the West River at Jamaica, and archaeological digs have been conducted in the Otter Creek area, at East Creek near Mt. Independence, at Swanton, at St. Albans, and elsewhere. There is no county in Vermont which has not produced Indian remains. To contribute to the body of knowledge of Vermont's Indian history, finds should be reported to the anthropology department of the University of Vermont.

2. *Champlain Arrives — 1609*

Unless some unrecorded Viking wandered into Vermont earlier, Samuel de Champlain was Vermont's first white visitor when he sailed up the inland lake that now bears his name. He had agreed to help the Algonquin Indians in their fight against the Iroquois, a gesture his French nation was later to regret.

According to Samuel Eliot Morison, Champlain's latest biographer, he was a man of virtuous character, loyal to his King Louis XIV and his church, sympathetic with the "savages," brave, and imaginative. He left us with some quaint self-portraits, valuable maps of New France, fascinating journals, and notes on the North American flora and fauna which he loved.

Champlain, not the first of the French explorers of Canada but its most famous, came into the area that is now Vermont

5

as a 42-year-old seasoned seaman who had explored the West Indies, Mexico, the New England shores, and Canada. He was determined to extend the boundaries of New France, and when the Abnakis of the Algonquin group, who had been driven out of the lake area by the Iroquois, suggested a venture into the land, Champlain was their man.

He left Quebec in June of 1609 with a party that grew to 49 Frenchmen and 300 Algonquins. But after a false start, Champlain trimmed the party to 60 Indians and two French volunteers. On July 3 this band entered the lake in canoes. In his journal Champlain faithfully estimated the size and recorded the lakeside growth, but he mistook marble outcroppings on a mountainside for snow. On July 29 his party met the Iroquois. Champlain wore shining armor and a white plume in his helmet, reminiscent of his days as a soldier in the Army of France.

On signal from the Abnaki leader, Champlain advanced and shot with his "arquebus" the three Iroquois chiefs in the forefront. Two were killed instantly, and the other one died later. The Iroquois rained arrows on the enemy, but no French or Algonquins were killed. The fight probably took place at what is now Crown Point.

Champlain's account of the voyage makes today's reader believe that they landed at Colchester Point, explored the Winooski River, and camped at Chimney Point and at the mouth of Otter Creek.

Champlain was sickened by the heinous behavior of the Algonquins toward the Iroquois prisoners, but he was unable to control the cruelty. The hatred of the Iroquois toward the French continued until the conquest of Canada by the British in 1760.

A man who did not follow the general custom of seducing the Indian girls, Champlain was something of an oddity. However, he did marry, when he was 40 years old, a 12-year-old Parisian girl, agreeing that he would not consummate the marriage for two years. Eventually he brought his Helene to Quebec, where she was undoubtedly very unhappy. After her husband's death in Quebec in 1635, she entered a convent in

France, childless.

Champlain never visited his lake again, but later the French established trading posts in his footsteps. One of Champlain's important accomplishments was a general map of North America he drew in 1612, showing Lake Champlain and the area from Labrador and Nova Scotia to Lake Ontario and New York. In his journal, as well as in other old records, the lake is referred to as the Lake of the Iroquois, indicating that Champlain renamed it for himself.

This quaint and disproportionate map, decorated with fruits and vegetables, charming whales, and "savages," is now in the Harvard College Library, probably the earliest map which shows the land of present day Vermont.

3. Jesuits and Father Jogues — 1638-46

Champlain's visit to Vermont was not immediately followed by other Frenchmen, but the French now considered this their territory. Champlain had made enemies of the Iroquois, and the land was still too dangerous for Europeans to make settlements. Some French trappers made use of the St. Lawrence, however, the Richelieu River, and Lake Champlain to get themselves further into the center of the country with the help of their allies, the Algonquins, because everybody who was anybody in Europe in the seventeenth century had to have a beaver hat and the Indian trappers and French traders provided the pelts.

The French traders and soldiers who came to the new settlements of Quebec and Montreal were soon followed by Jesuits who aspired to convert the Indians.

The Jesuits kept detailed and accurate records of their activities and have provided American and Canadian historians with rich material in their *Jesuit Relations*.

After Champlain's visit in 1609, the next recorded overnight European visitor in Vermont was Father Jogues. Born

Isaac Jogues in Orleans, France, in 1607, he was ordained in 1636 after the usual splendid education of a Jesuit. He came immediately to New France as a missionary to the Indians and served at the Great Lakes Huron mission from 1638 to 1642. Hurons were of the friendly Algonquin group.

But he yearned to convert his enemy, the dreaded Iroquois. His chance came. In August of 1642 Father Jogues was travelling from Quebec to his mission, accompanied by two lay brothers, when they were attacked by the Iroquois. Father Jogues could have escaped, as he was apart from his companions, but in keeping with his religious ideals he rushed into the fray to try to save his brothers and aid the dying Indians. He was, of course, captured and had to undergo heinous tortures, mutilation of the hands, ripped out fingernails, and other classic customs of the victors. This stopover has been credited as "the establishment of a mission."

Father Jogues reported that they were forced to endure "the salvo," which was a "game" of running prisoners between two rows of conquerors "each discharging a stick." He called it "the narrow road to Paradise." In the midst of his suffering, Father Jogues baptized two candidates with drops of dew from the stalk of a plant. He reported that he heard the confessions of the converts as they burned at the stake.

For 13 months Father Jogues was a slave in an Indian family. Finally he was ransomed by a Lutheran clergyman, the Rev. Jan Megapolensis, and a Dutch merchant, and returned to France via Manhattan. But Father Jogues had not lost his passion for converting the Indians. He returned to Quebec in 1646 and got permission to try to establish a mission with the Mohawks, of the Iroquois nation. Enroute he camped again at Isle LaMotte and at Otter Creek.

At first things went well. He had brought gifts from the King of France, and the Mohawks seemed friendly. Then an epidemic developed after a church celebration, following which caterpillars destroyed much of the Indian grain. Father Jogues was accused of sorcery and horribly tortured by the angry and fearful Mohawks. On October 18, 1646,

Father Jogues and his companions had their heads torn from their bodies and exposed on palisades in the village.

At least that happened on the New York side of Lake Champlain — to the possible credit of the history of Vermont.

4. French Forts and Soldiers — 1665-71

The first settlement by Europeans in what is now Vermont was on Isle LaMotte in 1665. Fifty-eight years before the first English settlement was made at Brattleboro's Fort Dummer, the French built Fort Ste. Anne. Three French forts for fighting the Indians had already been built further up on the Richelieu River, but they wanted an outpost reaching into Lake Champlain as well. Isle LaMotte was the logical spot since Iroquois, Algonquins, trappers, missionaries, and explorers crossed and recrossed that area.

Jean-Baptiste Le Gardineur de Repentigny went from Quebec with 20 men in October 1665 to determine an exact site, choosing the sandy point on the north shore of the island, but construction had to wait until spring. The new fort was to be dedicated to Sainte Anne, the mother of the Virgin Mary, despite its purpose to wipe out Indians.

About 300 men of the Carignan Regiment under Sieur de la Motte were assigned to the fort, which was completed on July 20, 1666. M. Dubois, chaplain of the regiment, had celebrated the first mass in Vermont at the moment of dedication of the site, probably in early May. On July 26, 1666, in the presence of the soldiers the new fort was formally dedicated to Sainte Anne with another religious ceremony. Old records and archaeological work done by the Roman Catholic church in Vermont some years ago reveal that the fort was 144 feet long and 96 feet wide, with a double palisade 15 feet high and four bastions.

The English down in New England were uneasy and enraged by the whole procedure. Governor Winthrop of

Connecticut sent spies to Lake Champlain. The spies reported that during construction the weather was good and that life at the fort was gay, with hunting parties, abundant fish, and enough danger from the Indians to make life exciting. The Chazy River near the fort was named for M. de Chasy, a highly connected and popular French officer who was killed by the Indians while on a hunting expedition from the fort.

The French planned a great campaign into western Indian country. Actually, they succeeded in making a short peace with the Mohawks, but by November 1666, after vicious and unresolved fighting, the operation closed as deep snow had cut off the fort. Sixty soldiers were trapped there for the winter, 40 of whom had scurvy, for the French had refused to heed the Indian remedies for warding it off. Good Catholics all, they were in despair at having no priest and death all around.

Father Dollier de Casson, a Jesuit of superior mental and physical power, volunteered at once to go down from Quebec on snowshoes despite "a swelling of the knee." A number of lives were saved by his presence and by the supplies he brought, including "salt, purslane, onions, fowl, capon, and a vast quantity of prunes." As far as anyone knows, the first letter written in Vermont was by Father de Casson.

In the spring of 1667 peace was made with the Iroquois, who asked for missionaries. Life was good again, and the number of soldiers was greatly reduced. When Louis XIV of France wanted more soldiers for his war in Europe, he recalled the Carignan Regiment to France.

There seem to have been no more soldiers at Fort Ste. Anne after 1671, according to historian Guy Coolidge.

Today, the Vermont Official Highway Map shows the Shrine of Ste. Anne, and an official Vermont Historic Site marker at Isle LaMotte indicates that here was Vermont's first white settlement.

5. French Seigniories — 1696-1759

The story of the French efforts to colonize the Champlain Valley has been known and told by few people. France claimed Lake Champlain due to Champlain's discovery of it, and as early as 1696 Louis XIV of France gave an order to begin granting seigniories, or land tracts, along the St. Lawrence, the Richelieu River, and Lake Champlain.

The seigniory plan was based on the old feudal system, with the lord or seigneur owing direct homage to the king and his tenants owing fealty to the lord, with obligations and rewards on both sides. This was the basic French colonization pattern and existed in some form in Canada until 1854.

The king decreed that the persons who held these grants must get them under cultivation and bring in settlers. Grandiose old Louis had in mind a great French empire in North America, the nucleus of which would be naturally bounded by the St. Lawrence, the Connecticut River, and Lake Ontario. He had only to fear the English to the south. In 1684 map makers indicated the frontier of New France at the southern end of Lake Champlain, and Louis envisioned a great city on its shore.

Yet settlement was poor. Huguenots who wanted to come were not permitted, and colonists were afraid of the English and the Iroquois. They were not allowed to own land outright, and they did not have the freedom or incentives to make homes in the wilderness that the English colonists had.

Nevertheless, colonization by the French did take place in Vermont. From a French map published by De Lery in 1748 but surveyed in 1732, it appears that seven large seigniories existed on Lake Champlain's eastern shores.

Fort Chambly on the Richelieu River already existed for protection, and in 1731 the French built a small stockaded fort at Crown Point and called it Fort St. Frederick. Later it was enlarged, made the strongest fortress on the lake, and settlements sprang up around it. About 1740 a French set-

11

tlement began in what is now Windmill Point, Alburg, on the grant of Sieur Francis Foucault. He established a few settlers and built a stone windmill which cost $800. Evidently he meant to stay, for the windmill was standing many years later. M. Foucault also built a church, but the colony did not prosper or last.

The southernmost of the seigniories was owned by Sieur Gilles Hocquart. He obtained the grant in 1743 in the area of Ferrisburg, Addison, Vergennes, and Middlebury. Included here is Chimney Point opposite Fort St. Frederick, which was a substantial settlement. The settlement here probably went back to the days of the construction of Fort Ste. Anne in 1666.

In 1730 there was a French village at Chimney Point, which had a population of about 300, and which lasted until they were driven out by the British in 1759. The French burned all their buildings when the British came, giving it the name Chimney Point, as chimneys were all that were left behind.

Peter Kalm (1715-1779), a person to intrigue the imagination, was a Swedish naturalist and professor who came to America to study the country, arriving at Lake Champlain in 1749. Later he wrote a book, *A Naturalist's Tour in North America*, leaving us some knowledge of the French settlements.

The French provided the only real settlements in Vermont from 1609, when Champlain came, to the final defeat of France in North America, a period of 150 years.

6. *King Philip's War — 1665-67*

Before Vermont had any European settlers, one regional Indian affair that affected the area was King Philip's War of 1665-1667. King Philip was an Indian whose real name was Metacom, son of the great sachem Massosoit of the Wampanoag Tribe of Rhode Island. The English "christened" him Philip. That Philip was a man of intelligence and kingly qualities is evident.

Massosoit (and in turn Philip) ruled the New England Indians of Massachusetts and Rhode Island, including the Pocassets, Narragensetts, Nipmucks, and others who formed a loose confederation. Massosoit got along well with the English and aided the struggling colonists, but Philip assessed the situation more practically. He saw that the Indian lands were fast being taken by the increasing number of colonists. By 1670 he saw the pressure on hunting grounds, fishing streams, and corn fields, realizing that the Indians were always at a disadvantage with the Europeans. In most cases the whites imposed their laws, customs, and religion with no thought of their bigotry and intolerance, regarding the Indians as "heathens."

Nothing angered Philip more than the colonists' determination to change the Indian religion, despite the good intentions of such men as John Eliot, who translated the Bible into an Indian tongue. (But of course Indians were further divided by many tribal tongues of their own, a great deterrent to Indian unity.) Philip bitterly resented the Indians who had been converted and educated and had come back to preach to their own people. It was one of these Indians, John Sassamon, who discovered that Philip was plotting to unite the Indians to exterminate the English and took the story to Plymouth authorities. Philip had Sassamon executed by tribal council.

Weetamoo, a brave Indian squaw-sachem who ruled her people, the Saconets, joined Philip in inciting the Indians with war dances and incantations. The young Indians were inflamed, and uneasy colonists mustered troops to "put down" the disturbance, not comprehending that there would be a general war.

Furious fighting developed on both sides, with numbers of colonists and Indians slaughtered. There was terror, blood, meanness, and treachery as Indians were induced to fight Indians. Meantime, the French Canadians were fomenting Catholic Indian warfare against Protestant Indians and whites in New England, who, it must be noted, tried to do the same thing to the French.

The English, determined to kill Philip, ordered a mass

dragnet to capture him. They killed his wife and children and closest followers. Philip was finally betrayed by one of his own tribesmen, who was angry at Philip for killing his brother who had suggested seeking peace. He led an Englishman to Philip's hideaway where he tried to shoot the sleeping chief, but his gun did not go off. In the end it was the treacherous Indian who fired the fatal shot at King Philip on August 12, 1676.

After Philip's death fighting continued, but a year later the Indians surrendered.

The embittered remnants of Philip's army are said to have moved north to the site of the present town of Vernon, where they camped until it became too dangerous. Most of them moved north through Vermont and joined other Indians at the north end of Lake Champlain and on Missisquoi Bay. Later this group came to be known as the St. Francis Indians, converted by the Jesuits. Their descendants figured largely in Indian raids on English settlements in the French and English struggle for supremacy in North America.

Just as most of the early Indians were kind to the white settlers, so were some whites filled with shame at the manner in which Indians were treated. An old book by Samuel Drake in the Vermont State Library states:

"Had every white Inhabitant who fat himfelf down by the Side of an Indian been kind and generouf, difcovererd lefs of Avarice, and not taken Pains to make himfelf offenfive by hif unmistakble Haughtinefs, few cafes of contention would have arifen."

7. King William's War — 1689-97

The colonial wars in North America called the French and Indian wars lasted from 1689 to 1762, with four phases punctuated by short periods of peace. They were King William's

War (1689-97, called War of the League of Augsburg, in Europe); Queen Anne's War (1702-13, called the War of Spanish Succession in Europe); King George's War (1744-48, called the War of Austrian Succession in Europe); the French and Indian War (1755-62, called the Seven Years' War in Europe).

Remote as they may seem today, these wars were of vast importance to the territory that would eventually become Vermont, which, unlike its neighboring states, was never a colony of England. There were no English settlers on Vermont's land before 1724, but the New England colonists whose descendants would settle Vermont in time were deeply involved in the French-English-Indian struggle.

In the sixteenth and seventeenth centuries, because of Cartier's and Champlain's explorations, France claimed Canada, the St. Lawrence, and Lake Champlain. The British claimed the Atlantic seaboard from Maine to Spanish Florida, thanks to Cabot's explorations. It was inevitable that French and English boundaries would meet, and that the enmities of Europe would blossom with a new kind of flower here.

Generally speaking, the English allied with the Iroquois, and the French with the Algonquins, who had been "christianized" to hate the English by zealous Jesuit missionaries. The notorious Indian raids against the English Protestant frontier settlements were part of these wars.

William of Orange came to the British throne in 1689, to the annoyance of King Louis XIV of France. William was a Protestant and a Dutchman, and Catholic Louis, who had been a king for 60 years since he was five years old, was easily whipped into a royal rage. He went to war with England and sent some French troops to Canada to beat the tar out of the New England English colonists who were spoiling for a fight as they watched the French move their frontier further south along Lake Champlain. King William's War began in all its savage brutality, with both sides arming their Indian allies.

The gruesome legends of Indians scalping women, debraining babies, and torturing men abound; each team used their Indians for the sickening slaughter that took place. To begin with, the Iroquois and English defeated the French at Lake Ontario, which so offended the domineering Colonial French Governor Frontenac that 210 French Canadians and Algonquins came "up" (meaning south) Lake Champlain on the ice in the winter of 1690 and attacked Schenectady, New York, and killed 60 people, including 11 Negro slaves. They burned the houses and took 27 captives.

To get even, the people of Albany with the help of the Mohawks set off to kill the French. This unpleasantness caused some intercolonial cooperation, and General Sir William Phips from Boston sailed up to Port Royal (Nova Scotia) to kill some of the French colonists. Phips had been an adventurer who made a great fortune by salvaging a wrecked treasure ship of the Spanish Plate Fleet. For this ingenuity he had been knighted and, joining Cotton Mather's church in Boston, he became very respectable.

This did not stop Phips from desecrating the French church, plundering the town, and forcing the Canadians to take an oath of allegiance. He brought back 27 captives, who were valuable as they could be swapped off for English prisoners.

Captures and reprisals like this went on for years. "Christian" Indians, using Lake Champlain for a route, plundered, burned, and pillaged in Maine and New Hampshire. One "French" Indian captive, Chief Bomaseen, was brought to Boston. He said he was a Christian and that he knew that the Virgin Mary was a French lady whose son Jesus was murdered by Englishmen, and that he had risen to Heaven, and all who wanted to earn favor must avenge his death.

What ended the war? There was a truce in Europe that included North America, news reaching these shores months later. Who won? Nobody. Dead were 650 English colonists, 300 French, and about 1300 Indians. The mutual feeling was that there would be no peace in North America until one or the other team was completely obliterated.

8. Queen Anne's War — 1702-13

Although the treaty in 1697 in Europe decreed peace between the French and the British, in America it was an uneasy agreement. By 1702 Louis XIV was at it again; he didn't like the choice of the King of Spain, so the War of Spanish Succession broke out in Europe, and England and France being, of course, on different sides sent word to their colonists that they should go to war again. Here it was called Queen Anne's War (1702-1713) because she had recently ascended the British throne.

The Iroquois had managed to make a separate peace with the French in the last round, so this time they were quiet. Canada hesitated to make New York angry again, so this time Lake Champlain was not used as a route for attacking the Yorkers. Instead, the French and their Abnaki-Algonquin allies, who were being run out of Maine and settling in great numbers around the northern end of Lake Champlain, used what is now Vermont as a great highway to get to the colonists in Massachusetts.

Louis, eager to have a greater Candian fur market, sent massive help from France. Not to be outdone, new Queen Anne sent troops to look after England's interests.

Some of this war was fought in the South for a change, where the Creek Indian nation was stirred up to kill off the white settlers there. By this time French explorers were working on encircling the British colonies and were making strides in the Great Lakes and Mississippi River regions. The British colonists were alarmed.

In New England the French led off by joining the Abnakis to raid Wells, Saco, and Casco in Maine, with the usual carnage, but to Vermont the most significant raid of this war was the sack of Deerfield, Massachusetts, the major northern settlement on the Connecticut River. It had 41 houses and kept up a constant guard which unfortunately did not work efficiently on the night of February 29, 1704.

The French and Indians under Captain Hertel de Rouville burned and killed and then took 111 prisoners to walk up the present State of Vermont on a 300-mile trip to Montreal. Understandably, they did not all survive the journey. A famous captive, the Rev. John Williams, wrote a best-selling book of the experience, *The Redeemed Captive*. On Sunday, March 5, the company rested near the present town of Rockingham, and the Reverend Williams preached what is undoubtedly the first Protestant sermon in Vermont.

The Reverend Mr. Williams' wife and baby died and other children were forcibly separated from him on the march. Three sons and two daughters survived with him and were eventually ransomed, but daughter Eunice could not be bought away from the Indians. She remained with the Caunawaga converts, turned Catholic, married an Indian, and had two children. Thirty-six years later she was reunited with her family, but she didn't get along with them, returned to the Indians and lived to be an 89-year-old squaw.

Naturally, troops were raised for reprisals. The British Crown finally sent a fleet under Adm. Hovenden Walker. Col. Francis Nicholson, a colonial, took troops by way of Lake Champlain so they could converge on Quebec. Admiral Walker considered the assignment beneath him, so he botched it and got badly beaten in the St. Lawrence fracas; even some of the women on his warships were killed. Colonel Nicholson was so mad he is said to have torn off his wig and stamped on it in a rage on the Lake Champlain shore. It cheered him up later to learn that Walker was dismissed from the navy for poor conduct.

Quebec thanked God for deliverance. When Boston received the news it coincided with a dreadful fire. The Rev. Increase Mather told his congregation it was because they had worked on Sunday preparing for Walker's expedition. They quaked, fearing a French reprisal.

The Treaty of Utrecht in Europe ended this war as mysteriously, to Americans, as it began; but this was not the end of the French and British colonial fighting.

9. Fort Dummer and the Equivalent Lands — 1715-24

At the time of the end of Queen Anne's War colonial land boundaries were vague at best. In 1713 when Connecticut and Massachusetts Bay Colonies tried to clarify their perimeters it was discovered that Massachusetts had made grants of land that properly belonged to Connecticut, with a total of 107,793 acres involved. By the time the land had been granted and settled, the indignant inhabitants had no desire to change colonial allegiance from Massachusetts to Connecticut. So the former agreed to give the latter an equal amount of land which she could sell and pocket the price.

A joint commission from the two colonies was appointed, and by 1715 they had laid out tracts which included "43,973 acres within the Limits of the Second Province on the Connecticut River." This large unsettled tract lay in the present towns of Putney, Dummerston, and Brattleboro. Known as "the equivalent lands," it was here that the first English settlements in Vermont were made.

In April of 1716 the land was sold at auction by Connecticut in Hartford at "a little more than a farthing an acre" to 21 persons from Massachusetts, Connecticut, and London, England, who paid 683 pounds New England currency.

The Colony of Connecticut, now richer in cash, although she had gained no land, gave the money to Yale College. In the partition of the land purchase the Vermont section became the property of William Dummer, William Brattle, Anthony Stoddard, and John White, and it was technically part of the Massachusetts Bay Colony.

William Dummer, for whom Fort Dummer and Dummerston were named, was evidently an affable man who, as Lieutenant Governor of Massachusetts, soothed the people and acted as a tactful buffer between them and the cantankerous Governor Samuel Shute. Dummer, although an official and a land owner, like all frontier settlers was concerned with safety from French and Indian forays. An old Appleton's *Cyclopaedia of Biography* says that "Dummer conducted the Indian War with energy and the affairs of the province were administered with wisdom and impartiality."

As acting executive head of the Massachusetts government in 1724, he appointed Col. John Stoddard of Northampton to select a site for a fort and to superintend its construction.

Colonel Stoddard wrote back to Lieutenant Governor Dummer in February 1724 and mentioned that he had ordered snowshoes and moccasins for the workers, that he had appointed Lt. Timothy Dwight as builder, and that 12 soldiers, four carpenters, and two teams of horses would work with him. They would hew the timber and construct the fort and necessary houses during the month of February.

The carpenters were paid five shillings a day except for an Indian carpenter, Johnny Crowfoot, who got six shillings a day because the other carpenters agreed that he worked harder than the rest. The soldiers received extra pay for the hard assignment.

The fort, built of yellow pine logs, was about 180 feet square. The sides of the fort were the backs of the dwellings which were built inside the walls. Costing 256 pounds, it was near the present town of Brattleboro on the west bank of the Connecticut River. The actual site is flooded since the building of the dam at Vernon, but now Fort Dummer State Park commemorates the spot.

10. Life at Fort Dummer — 1724-26

Timothy Dwight, the builder of Fort Dummer, was made captain of the 55 soldiers of the garrison which was installed at the opening of the fort in June 1724. Forty-three of the soldiers were English colonials, but the remaining 12 were

"Maquos" Indians, Mohawks from New York State. Capt. Joseph Kellog had been sent out to Albany to negotiate for the services of the Indians.

Great effort was made by Massachusetts to have good relations with the Indians. Three of the Indian recruits were sachems, the most famous of whom was Hendrick Maqua; another was Umpaumet. The list of Indians serving at the fort does not indicate who the third sachem was. The sachems were given extra pay of two shillings a day, and the agreement went on to say that "none of ye Indians be stinted as to allowance of provisions; That they all have the use of their arms gratis, and their guns mended at free cost; That a supply of knives, pipes, tobacco, lead, shot, and flints, be sent to the commanding officer at the forts, to be given out to them, according to his discretion." The Indians were also to be given one gill of rum a day. But even with these inducements the Indians did not want to stay over a year.

The English at the fort were concerned for the morals of the Indians; Massachusetts provided a chaplain to christianize them, with what success it is not recorded.

Despite raids and fights with the Indians from Canada, the presence of Fort Dummer brought relative peace to the area. In 1727 a trading post was established at the fort for the benefit of the Indians as well as the colony. This was a further step to insure friendship with the Indians, since it was an outlet for their furs and a way for them to obtain food and clothing and other trade goods. The "Truck House" was for many years part of the establishment.

Capt. Samuel Partridge, among others, was concerned that the Indians were sometimes cheated by trading liquor for furs, so regulations were put into effect providing more justice for the Indians. Captain Kellog was in charge of the trading post, and he appears to have done a good job, making the place profitable and popular with both Indians and white traders.

Meantime, families had come to live inside the fort. To one of these huts young Captain Dwight brought his wife, and here on May 27, 1726, was born the first English child re-

21

corded in Vermont. It was a sturdy boy baby named Timothy. He grew to be 6'4", unusual for that day, and was "very strong." He graduated from Yale in 1744 and became a prominent merchant and citizen of Northampton. He was a loyalist during the Revolution and died in Natchez, Mississippi in 1777. He had married Mary Edwards, daughter of the famous preacher Jonathan Edwards. They had thirteen children, the eldest of whom was the president of Yale from 1795 to 1817.

Other forts were gradually built in the area: Sartwell's Fort, two miles south of Fort Dummer, a small fortified residence built in 1738; and Fort Bridgman, built in the present town of Vernon at about the same time. These forts made it possible for settlers to begin looking at the green land of Vermont.

11. *Sebastian Rale's War — 1713-24*

Sebastian Rale's War, sometimes called Governor Dummer's War, in the interval of "peace" between 1713 and 1744, was a messy example of colonial barbarity which had an effect on Vermont since it involved the Abnaki Indians.

Sebastian Rale (or Rasle or Ralle) was a tough and brilliant French Jesuit who arrived in Quebec in 1689 with political aggression as well as religion on his mind. He immediately began to learn the Indian language and went out to live with the St. Francis Indians in northern Vermont in the present Swanton area, where the Abnakis and the remnants of King Philip's army had established a village.

Father Rale, according to Abby Hemenway, was the terror of New England in his bitter determination to drive out the English settlers. In 1695 he went to Maine as a missionary to the Abnakis at Norridgewock on the Kennebec, where the Indians already had a Roman Catholic church. So zealous were they that when they moved down to the sea to fish they took a tent-like tabernacle along for services. Father Rale got many more new converts. Hemenway thought this controversial man was a hero, but a rare old book, *A History of the Indian Wars* by E. Hoyt, published in 1824, gave a different picture.

For background: at the end of Queen Anne's War Acadia was ceded to the English. The French said this meant only Nova Scotia, but the English said it meant all the Maritime Provinces. Since the Kennebec was the dividing line for the frontier, it was decided in disgruntled French political councils to put Father Rale in this critical spot to incite the Abnakis to fight the English, providing a living barrier.

Historian Francis Parkman says that great changes came over the Jesuits of this period. He praised the earlier dedicated missionaries, but he had no sympathy for Sebastian Rale with his caustic tongue, strong body, and unequivocal determination to convert the Indians.

The infuriated English retaliated with total rage. Father Rale says they put a reward of 1000 pounds sterling on his head, but there is no substantiation for this. The English raised 300 men to go to Norridgewock to demand that the Indians give up Rale. They did not get the priest, but papers fell into English hands showing without doubt Rale's political intrigue.

In 1717 when Governor Shute of Massachusetts called the Indians to a council at Arrowsick Island they came peacefully. The Puritans had decided that they should attempt to turn the Indians into Protestants and offered bonuses to ministers to preach Calvinism to the "heathens." Thus persuaded, the Rev. Joseph Baxter came to this convention and gave each Indian a Bible, which the Indians declined to accept. The Puritan efforts were hopeless. In his scornful correspondence, Father Rale ranted about Baxter, whom he despised.

Fitful fighting went on. In 1725 the Massachusetts Assembly disagreed with the governor and refused to fund the war. Governor Shute went to England to get help, leaving the whole messy affair in the hands of the more genial Lieutenant Governor Dummer, who persuaded the Assembly to raise the money.

The expedition was successful, for when the Massachusetts fighters got to Norridgewock they took the Indians by surprise. They found Father Rale in one of the houses madly firing his gun. Called on to surrender, the priest kept firing until he was shot through the head, although orders had been given that Rale should not be killed.

The *Jesuit Relations* give a different story. Sebastian Rale was a martyr to the French Canadians and an ogre to the English.

12. *King George's War — 1744-48*

In June 1743, an episode in Europe caused the third formal chapter in the French and Indian Wars. King George II of England, leading his troops through Holland (the last British monarch to appear at the head of an army), was attacked by a French army although the two countries were nominally at peace. War was declared between them in March 1744, a nasty conflict that became King George's War here.

It normally took two months to get word to the colonies. This time the French got the message first and immediately sent a force from Louisbourg to capture the English Acadian port of Canseau. The surprised troops surrendered on the condition that they be sent back to Boston.

The French agreed, taking them to Louisbourg en route. This enabled the English to see how vulnerable was the fortification. So by 1745 New England troops and British Navy vessels were planning a joint attack on Louisbourg. Command of the expedition was given to William Pepperrell of Kittery, Maine, a popular and prosperous 49-year-old merchant.

Boston was on fire with war fever, supported by the Puritan clergy who wanted the popish French driven out of North

America. It was indeed supported by everyone, as the years of French and French-inspired Indian raids on the expanding colonies kept up a fury of hatred, and troops were easily raised. This time the British Navy under Commodore Peter Warren came through with three 40-gun warships to cooperate with the New England forces.

With incredible luck they took Louisbourg on June 17, 1745. Colonial leadership of local militia had succeeded, and wild celebrations took place in the colonies. Warren was promoted to admiral and made governor of Louisbourg, and Pepperrell was made a baronet, the first native-born American to achieve this honor.

But the victory was hollow, because it was hard to maintain Louisbourg, and in the rest of New England terrible French and Indian raids began again. The Iroquois, who had been declared British subjects since 1713, were largely indifferent to pleas for help against the Abnakis, although some of the chiefs did go to Maine to try to win their friendship, with no success.

An added threat was the French construction of Fort St. Frederick at Crown Point in 1731. Massachusetts built three new forts between the Connecticut River and the New York line and posted 440 men on its northwest frontier.

Present Putney, Vermont, and Keene, New Hampshire, were attacked as well as Fort Number Four at Charlestown, New Hampshire, where Sgt. John Hawks surrendered on condition that his people become prisoners of the French, not the Indians. The French captain broke his word, but the Indians did not harm the prisoners this time.

Fighting continued in Acadia and on the frontier. Finally, even the Iroquois acted when Chief Hendrick, one of the sachems from Fort Dummer's early days, led a group of 40 up the St. Lawrence. In 1748 Capt. Eleazer Melvin took 18 men from Fort Dummer on a scouting expedition to Lake Champlain. Indians and Indian fighters stirred constantly in the frontier territory that is now Vermont.

The Treaty of Aix-la-Chapelle which ended the war was signed October 18, 1748, and news of it reached Boston in

December. The colonists were enraged at one of the terms: Louisbourg was to be returned to France! After its first great colonial military success America was insulted.

13. Indian Captives — 1689;1763

It is estimated that nearly 1200 captives from New England were taken to Canada for ransom during the French and Indian wars.

The French Indians, usually from St. Francis, would capture entire families and walk them through Vermont and canoe them to Canada by Lake Champlain. They would then be sold to the French, who generally treated them gently, and if they survived they could be ransomed, at a profit to the owner, by the families or colonial governments or by popular subscription.

Upon capture, each prisoner would be assigned to a squaw or brave, called mother or master, who would be responsible for the life and care of the charge. The Indian masters were paid in the transaction, so for that reason and through good nature the Indians seem to have treated most of the prisoners decently. Some prisoners never came back because they preferred to live with the Indians, especially children who spent many years in captivity.

A Narrative of the Captivity of Mrs. Johnson, published in 1796, is a hair-raising account of a kidnapping. Before dawn on August 30, 1754, during an interval of alleged peace, St. Francis Indians appeared at Fort Number Four at Charlestown, New Hampshire, and broke into the house of James Johnson. The Johnsons and neighbors had been partying the night before to celebrate the return of Mr. Johnson from Massachusetts.

Mr. Johnson opened the door to let in a hired helper, and along with the helper came a band of Indians who swarmed through the house and routed the naked Mrs. Johnson from her bed. She was allowed to put on a dress, and the entire family of parents, three small children, a sister, and two male neighbors, who had slept there for the night, were seized.

The Indians and their prisoners set out at once for Canada. Mrs. Johnson was in the last stages of pregnancy, and the next morning she was delivered of a daughter, whom she named Captive. They halted for a day for this event and then marched on, Mrs. Johnson being carried on a litter by the Indians. They finally captured a horse for her to ride, but it had to be killed for food, and little Captive was fed on well-chewed horse meat. The journey was incredibly hard, Mr. Johnson carrying his wife on his back much of the way.

In nine days they reached Crown Point, where they were well treated by the French. The children were fussed over and the new baby decked out in the latest French clothes, but on the fourth day they were returned to the Indians and taken by canoe to St. Francis. Eventually the prisoners were sold in Montreal to the French, but Mrs. Johnson, the baby, and one son were held in the Indian village until November, when Mrs. Johnson was sold to M. DuQuesne, who treated her kindly in his family. Meanwhile Mr. Johnson was given parole to raise money for ransom, but hardship followed hardship. The family was thrown into prison in Quebec city; they all contracted smallpox; one child was put in a nunnery; the boy was lost, not to be recovered for many years.

In 1758 they were all ransomed, but Mr. Johnson died shortly after they were released, fighting the French at Crown Point. Mrs. Johnson remarried and finally recovered all her children. Years later Mrs. Johnson erected two monuments near the spot where Captive was born. The stones are still standing at Felchville.

Perhaps Vermont's most famous Indian captive was Jemima Howe, who is buried in a well-marked grave which bears 23 lines in stone that tell her story, in the North Cemetery in Vernon.

Mrs. Howe did not write of her experiences for posterity, but she was sufficiently famous in her day that others wrote them for her. Called the "fair captive," she was reputedly an outstandingly beautiful and winning woman.

Jemima Howe and her second husband, Caleb, lived at Bridgman's Fort, near Fort Dummer, with their seven children and several neighbors. Her first husband, William Phipps, had been killed by Indians. On June 21, 1755, Mr. Howe and two of the sons were in the field near the fort when they too were attacked by the Indians. Caleb Howe was killed, but the women in the fort hearing shots, opened the doors for the men from the fields. Instead they admitted the Indians.

The Indians set fire to the fort, took all the women and children as captives, and set out for Canada. Mrs. Howe carried her six-month-old infant in her arms, but the baby died later. For eight days they marched to the shores of Lake Champlain where the Indian canoes were hidden. Mrs. Howe, like Mrs. Johnson, said the Indians were personally kind to them: "for such savage masters, in such indigent circumstances, we could not rationally hope for kinder treatment than we received," she told the Rev. Bunker Gay who wrote down her story.

This party was also detained at Crown Point by the French. A number of the prisoners, including some of the Howe children, were taken ahead to be sold to the French, and the Indians, not totally successful in their sales, gave one of the Howe daughters to Governor Vaudrieul. She later married a Frenchman and moved to France.

Mrs. Howe was separated from most of her children and sold to a Frenchman, who was kind and generous to her and took her home to his wife, but that triangle developed unhappily and the governor intervened in her behalf. A subscription was made by some kind-hearted Dutch and British people to buy her freedom, as she had no husband to act in her behalf. Later Mrs. Howe married Amos Tute, her third husband.

14. *The French and Indian War — 1755-62*

The last of the four declared struggles between the French and the English in North America was the French and Indian War (1755-1762). Often called the French War, it was the decisive one for British supremacy on this continent and the most important for the future state of Vermont, since it made the territory safe for settlement.

After the Treaty of Aix-la-Chapelle in 1748, hostilities were declared over, but the fighting in America between angry French and English colonists, and the Indians that both sides had inflamed, continued with unspeakable atrocities.

In the period between 1748 and 1755 the French expanded into the Ohio Valley and moved up from Louisiana, which not surprisingly, frightened and angered the English, who could see themselves cut off from westward expansion, perhaps even pushed into the Atlantic Ocean. It was at about this time that the Governor of Virginia sent 21-year-old Colonel George Washington and some Virginia militia to stop the French. Washington did not stop them, but he gained some valuable experience.

In 1756 in London, William Pitt, directing the war, saw that the way to stop France in Europe was to fight her in the colonies, and he set about at once to dispatch regular forces to the English colonies in America. Meantime, authorities in Paris decided to send French regulars to Canada.

In population, the English had a million and a quarter persons, and the French had 75,000, including the people of Louisiana, in North America.

In 1755 there were four major battles between colonial France and England, although they were not formally at war. Finally, on May 18, 1756, England declared war on France, which appears to have made it all legal. This time the war was supported almost entirely from London and Paris, and there were, predictably, problems on both sides between regular troops and local militia who distrusted each other.

The war was different in that the conflict started in America and spread to Europe, whereas the reverse had been true in the other colonial struggles.

The French had built Fort St. Frederick on Lake Champlain in 1731, and in 1755 they added Fort Carillon. That same year the English built Fort William Henry on Lake George and Fort Edward on the Hudson.

Also in 1755 a new commander-in-chief of the British forces in America arrived in Williamsburg, Virginia, Major General Edward Braddock, a 60-year-old professional soldier trained in European fighting. He was scornful of the colonial militia, but he was decisively defeated in Pennsylvania when he encountered French and Indian troops.

The 1863 Appleton's *Cyclopaedia of Biography* says he was "brave and able but unfortunate ... the disastrous event which has made his name memorable was owing to his contempt of the enemy. All his officers fell except George Washington and 700 were killed, including Braddock."

15. England Wins North America — 1763

The French command of the French and Indian War was given to General Louis Joseph de Montcalm, Marquis of St. Veran, a distinguished French general, in 1756. Obviously Europe was sending its finest to fight it out in America.

Montcalm has come down in history as a man much admired by his troops, his wife, his mother, and his ten bouncing children. Evidently his winning personality made the governor of New France, Marquis de Vaudreuil-Cavagnal, jealous to a memorable degree. The latter tried in every way to smear Montcalm, but Montcalm had the support of the Paris government. There was one serious blot on his good name, however. In 1757 he led the French from Fort Carillon to take Fort William Henry on Lake George from the English. The Canadian Indians in the victory committed hideous bar-

barities on the English prisoners who were shipped down Lake Champlain to Montreal and captivity. Montcalm did not or could not stop them. Some grisly stories of cannibalism and torture of the prisoners were recorded in old diaries, history books, and even in poems of the good old days.

In 1758 Major-General James Abercrombie was sent from England by William Pitt to capture Fort Carillon from the French. With his 15,000 troops, Abercrombie set out from Lake George and came north down Lake Champlain, with fanfare and flags flying, but they were wretchedly defeated by the French under Montcalm, with a slaughter of Scottish Black Watch troops sent on a hopeless assault on the fort. The colonial militia despised Abercrombie and dubbed him "Aunt Nabby Crombie."

Abercrombie was replaced by General Sir Jeffrey Amherst, a 41-year-old professional soldier whose command would eventually be vitally important to the future of Vermont. His first success was to capture Louisbourg with the help of General James Wolfe. In 1759 Amherst brought an army of regulars down Lake Champlain and captured Fort Carillon, thus gaining control of the lake. The French abandoned Fort St. Frederick, giving it to Amherst's troops. The French retreated north and partially blew up both forts, which were shortly renamed Fort Ticonderoga and Crown Point. Amherst then began to build up the latter.

When it became apparent that the French had been defeated in the Ohio Valley and on Lake Champlain and they had withdrawn to Canada, the English went all out for the capture of impregnable Quebec. For this task Pitt appointed General Wolfe, a gallant British officer who seems to have succeeded admirably in life despite a very receding chin. According to Appleton, "When that great minister the elder Pitt undertook in 1757 to raise the English from the temporary degradation into which she had fallen and to smite the house of Bourbon in every quarter of the globe he discerned the genius of Wolfe . . . and entrusted the young officer with the highest duties in the conquest of North America."

The story of how Wolfe in September 1759 found the secret

trail leading up to the city of Quebec is high adventure. When Montcalm awoke the next morning the British had ascended the Heights of Abraham. In the bloodiest battle of them all, both Wolfe and Montcalm were killed, both great men, both tragic losses as people and leaders.

Quebec fell, and later Montreal was taken by General Amherst. In 1763 the Treaty of Paris officially ended the war, and now North America belonged to the British.

And what was this to Vermont? When General Amherst made his plans to take Montreal he had a road built from Fort Number Four in Charlestown, New Hampshire, to Crown Point for moving troops through the wilderness. When peace came that road became Vermont's first highway.

Thirteen years later the British regulars who fought in North America would be the enemies of the colonists, but Amherst's road would be a reminder that British troops fought for as well as against the colonies.

16. Greylock — 1723-60

The Indians of the French and Indian wars seem mysterious, nameless, and faceless, but one legendary Indian burned the stamp of his personality so forcefully on the period that his name has not been forgotten.

Greylock, an Indian greatly feared by English settlers, was a proud chieftain of the Waranokes who in 1723 was living on the shores of Missisquoi Bay in a fort, or "castle" as it was called, that he had built for his band of followers. Called Greylock because of his gray hair, at this time he was an old man, having come from Massachusetts after the death of King Philip.

Greylock's castle was to become a legend. At about this time Fort Dummer was being built in the present region of Brattleboro, and Greylock was a mortal enemy of the English troops there. Although Lt. Gov. William Dummer of Massachusetts tried to conciliate Greylock and the other Indians living on the northern shores of Lake Champlain by sending belts and gifts, Greylock always made it a point to be absent when the messengers arrived.

Greylock killed, scalped, preyed upon travellers on Lake Champlain, and led raids on Northfield, Rutland, and Massachusetts frontier towns. In 1725 the English discussed organizing a large scouting party to try to destroy Greylock and his castle, but Lt. Col. John Stoddard, who selected the site of Fort Dummer, objected as he feared Indian reprisals. Chief Greylock was well supplied with guns by Governor Philippe Vaudreuil of Canada.

Finally Capt. Benjamin Wright raised a party of 59 rangers to fight it out with Greylock. Captain Wright kept a journal of the expedition entitled "A true journal of our march from N-field to Mesixcouk Bay under ye command of Benj. Wright Captain, begun July 27, A.D., 1725."

The party started out on the Connecticut River from Northfield, Massachusetts, and stopped at Fort Dummer to mend their canoes before proceeding to Bellows Falls, taking the familiar Indian water route, sometimes called the French Highway, that leads to Lake Champlain.

Failing to find Greylock's castle they returned home in September, but actually Greylock was not at his castle. In August he had left with a party of 150 Indians for the purpose of watching Captain Wright and harassing the Connecticut Valley towns.

When Governor Vaudreuil, who encouraged warfare, died in October of 1725, the Indians, weary of fighting, wanted to return to hunting and trapping. A peace treaty was signed between the English and the Eastern Indians in December 1725.

But Greylock wouldn't sign. In 1726 he assembled a war party at Otter Creek, but most Indians, peaceful people at heart, wouldn't accompany him at the last minute. The English tried hard to make peace with Greylock. As a friendly gesture, English colonial Indian commissioners invited him to Albany, but he refused.

Things were relatively peaceful in the Connecticut Valley for the next 18 years. There is no further record of this remarkable Indian whose vital career of resistance to the whites lasted 50 years.

Greylock's castle was as important in 1725 as Fort Dummer was, yet only Fort Dummer is remembered and marked by suitable monuments. Massachusetts named a mountain for him, but the exact site of Greylock's castle in Vermont is unknown.

17. Rogers' Rangers — 1755-63

Stories of the British and French and Indian conflicts are not complete without a tribute to the redoubtable Robert Rogers and his Rangers.

Born in Methuen, Massachusetts, in 1731, Rogers grew up on the frontier of Massachusetts and New Hampshire knowing the poverty, the fears, the hatreds, and the dangers of such a life. Large and sturdy and unschooled, he said he learned woodcraft from the Indians whom he later terrorized. At any rate he was a son of the wilderness, learning early to rely on himself and to be a match for any man in trading, fighting, and surviving.

His talents were immeasurably valuable to the times and the place. As a boy he saw his family homestead, after ten years of labor, burned by the Indians; the constant fear of Indian raids was his daily fare. It is no surprise that when Governor Shirley of Massachusetts sent out a call for men to join the attack on Nova Scotia, Rogers, then 24, was the man for the job. He went to work to recruit a company; in 1755 he brought in 50 men, and the regiment was officially activated with Rogers as captain and John Stark as lieutenant.

Probably more due to foolhardiness than to criminal enterprise, Rogers had been arrested for counterfeiting. The charge was dropped and in the excitement of the fight against Canada it was overlooked and never reopened.

Rogers soon established himself as a daring and bold Indian fighter. His heart was in it, he was strong, and he was able. Killing people didn't turn his stomach, and as a recruiter he was a success. In 1756 Governor William Shirley appointed him captain of an independent company of scouts who were to be an elite corps to gather intelligence, fight Indians, and perform commando raids whenever they could find a victim.

He was so successful that by 1758 he was made captain of nine such companies to head the scouting branch of the British army in America. These companies were made up of independent frontiersmen who did not respond well to military discipline and who preferred to operate with uninhibited and hazardous zeal.

The Rangers were and were not part of the army. Looking back on it, it would seem that the British regulars used them to do the dirty work, but the pay was good: three shillings a day for the men and ten shillings a day for Rogers, plus uniforms, arms, and blankets. The group was formed by the commanding general and paid by royal funds, but its existence could be terminated by whim of the general. They had to constantly prove their value, so they brought in scalps by the dozens. No, all scalping wasn't done by the Indians.

Rogers and his men fought a celebrated battle on snow-shoes with unbelievable courage, but he is probably best remembered for his destruction of the St. Francis Indians at their stronghold near present Swanton, sent by General Amherst. He killed 200 Indians and rescued six white captives in this final shoot-out; the 100 broken, surviving Indians scattered to live alone or join other tribes. It is a grim story, but on the other hand the frontier people had suffered such cruelties from this headquarters of the French Indians that Rogers was regarded as a holy savior by the folks back home. Certainly it opened the possibility of settlement in Vermont.

Rogers married Betsy Browne of Portsmouth, New Hampshire, whom he promptly deserted to fight Indians in the

South and West. A letter left by him indicates touchingly that he loved her very much, but she finally divorced him, getting custody of the one child, after years of separation and neglect.

With peace in 1763 there was no further need for such blood-thirsty fighters. Poor Rogers could not cope with peace. He enraged the authorities by allegedly holding traitorous dealings with the French, and in 1765 he went to England where he wrote his memoirs, and was hailed as a hero. He wrote a play, one of the first dramas by a native American, and tried to promote an expedition to the Northwest Passage with no luck.

He finally wound up in a British debtor's prison from which his brother bailed him out, and he returned to America. A Tory, he was arrested as a spy by George Washington, but he escaped and raised a company of the loyalist Queen's American Rangers. He fled to England in 1780 and died there in 1795 in a cheap lodging house.

18. Amherst's Road — 1759-60

Lord Jeffrey Amherst's Military Road was one of the most important legacies of the colonial war to the territory that would become Vermont.

When General Amherst seized the French forts on Lake Champlain in 1759, his aim was to take Montreal. A careful man, he wanted to leave no loopholes in the success of his plans, so he arranged to have a three-pronged attack on the city. The New Hampshire men who were to take part in the expedition met at Fort Number Four in Charlestown and instead of going to Crown Point by way of Albany as usual, they were commanded to cut a road across the land that is now Vermont, opening direct land communication between Lake Champlain and the Connecticut River.

This was not an entirely new idea. In 1756 the governor of

Massachusetts had requested the provincial assembly to appoint 14 men to measure the distance between Crown Point and Number Four. The request seemed reasonable and the route was surveyed, following the general path of an old Indian route. Shortly after he arrived at Crown Point General Amherst wrote to Gov. Benning Wentworth of New Hampshire to tell him that men were already cutting the road and that it should be finished in a few weeks, although it did not turn out to be that easy.

The work on what soon became known as the Military Road was begun by Capt. John Stark of New Hampshire who was later to be the hero of the Battle of Bennington. With 200 Rangers they began the clearing at Crown Point. After a few months Major John Hawks with 300 New England troops took over, felling trees, pulling stumps, and watching out for the Indians. By this time the French had withdrawn to Canada.

Major Hawks, whose part of the endeavor was to supervise the building of the road over the Green Mountains, left a diary, and a peak between Baltimore and Cavendish is named in his honor. In 1760 Lt. Col. John Goffe with 800 New Hampshire men was ordered to complete the road, and 44 days were spent cutting a road 26 miles long to the foot of the Green Mountains. Twenty-six mile posts were erected, some of which still exist on the old trail, which is kept partially identified by the Crown Point Road Association.

Colonel Goffe's regiment reached Crown Point on July 31, 1760, with a drove of cattle, just in time to join Col. William Haviland's forces for the attack on Montreal. The diary notes that an epidemic broke out while the eastern section of the road was being built, killing several men who were buried beside the road near present Springfield.

Starting at Chimney Point, opposite Crown Point, in the present town of Addison, the remains of the road roughly passes through Bridport, Shoreham, Whiting, Sudbury, Rutland Falls, Mount Holly, Plymouth, Ludlow, Cavendish, Weathersfield, to Charlestown.

The road immediately opened up the center of the territory.

Crude inns began to appear, and there was even the possibility of wagon travel from Lake Champlain to Boston. Who owned this land? New York? Massachusetts? New Hampshire? Problems loomed as fast as the possibilities.

19. Boundaries — 1720-64

Since Vermont was never a colony and since the boundaries of neighboring New York, New Hampshire, and Massachusetts colonies were dim and ill-defined, there was considerable confusion as to who owned this territory that was now opening up. Land was needed for expansion, and, with the new Military Road and relative peace with the Indians, Vermont beckoned.

When Massachusetts built Fort Dummer in 1724 some of the land in the region had been granted and the "equivalent lands" had been sold by Connecticut to a land company. New Hampshire and Massachusetts, although nominally two separate colonies, were united under one governor but had separate councils and legislatures. New Hampshire claimed the land on which Fort Dummer was built; Massachusetts countered by asking New Hampshire to maintain the fort. They did the job badly and Massachusetts, which stood to gain the most by the defense, took it over again. The matter rocked along like that for about 20 years until the king finally designated the boundary, where it lies today between Vermont and Massachusetts, giving New Hampshire more than she asked for. In that same year, 1741, New Hampshire got her first governor, a colorful man named Benning Wentworth.

Now the western boundary of Connecticut had been fixed at a line 20 miles east of the Hudson, so Massachusetts claimed her boundary that far west too. Then New Hampshire did the same, and in 1749 Governor Wentworth granted a township six miles square, just north of the Massachusetts line and 20 miles east of the Hudson. He named it for himself, calling it Bennington.

This was the beginning of a long list of grants made by Wentworth, mostly to rich people from Massachusetts or Connecticut who did not intend to settle the new land themselves but who sold lots to the hardy poor who wished to get a better deal out of life than was offered back home. In Bennington the governor held out 500 acres for himself, establishing a pattern which eventually made him a very rich man.

Between 1749 and 1754, a relatively peaceful period, Wentworth granted many more townships: Westminster, Dummerston, Putney, Brattleboro, Rockingham, Halifax, Newfane, Vernon, Marlboro, Wilmington, Springfield, Stamford, Townshend, Woodford, Chester, Grafton, and Guilford. Some of these were affirmations of grants made by Massachusetts. Settlements of sorts were made in most of them, which folded under mounting French and Indian pressure as war exploded again. No other grants were made until 1760, at which time the previously granted land renewed its settlements with peace at hand.

The pattern established by the Bennington grant was generally followed as new grants were made. In addition to the two shares or 500 acres set aside for the governor there was one share for the Society of the Propagation of the Gospel in Foreign Parts, one share for the Church of England, one share for the first settled minister, and one share for a school. An elective form of government was set up and a town meeting for election of officers was required on the last Wednesday in March; each grantee had to plant five acres of land for each 50 acres within five years and keep it in cultivation; all pine trees fit for masting for the British Navy must be preserved; a market was to be held when the population reached a certain size. Many friends of Wentworth were rewarded with lots.

By the end of 1764 Governor Wentworth had granted 131 townships, and the fees he charged for the transfer made him even richer. He was a real estate operator in a matchless situation of land speculation, but it would be folly to suppose

that he could keep this up forever. Over in New York colony
Lt. Gov. Cadwallader Colden, who had been surveyor general,
knew the value of the land and recognized a gravy train when
he saw it. What about the New York boundary? Colden knew
it was worth investigating.

20. Benning Wentworth, the Man —
1696-1776

In days when conniving politicians fill the papers, it is en-
lightening to examine some political shenanigans of the past.
The story of how Benning Wentworth, so important to early
Vermont history, became governor of New Hampshire and
subsequently the kingpin of land grants in the territory that
would become Vermont is worth telling.

Wentworth came from a powerful family, both in England
and in America where he was born in Portsmouth, New
Hampshire, in 1696. His father was Lieutenant Governor of
New Hampshire which at that time was nominally part of
Massachusetts despite its separate government. Young
Benning, characterized by Governor Jonathan Belcher of
Massachusetts as possessing "pertness" and "insolence and
ill manners," went straight into business with his father
after graduating from Harvard in 1715. The Wentworth family was involved in lumber trade with Spain, a magnificently
profitable arrangement whereby New Hampshire (and Vermont) timber went to Spain in exchange for Spanish wine and
British credit. Benning went often to Spain where he adopted
such haughty and genteel manners that he was called Don
Granada.

In 1730, after his father's death, he moved the family business headquarters from Boston to Portsmouth, a rich and
bustling town in those days. There he built himself a fine and
celebrated mansion.

In 1733 Benning Wentworth delivered a mighty shipment

of timber to the Spanish government in Cadiz, but as British and Spanish relations were pointing to war, which soon came, the Spanish refused to pay. Wentworth went bankrupt with a debt of 11,000 pounds, a huge sum of money for which he entered a claim against the British government.

Wentworth had an agent in London, John Thomlinson, who played a great role in the future of New Hampshire and Vermont. He called all the Wentworth creditors together in London and, after making them promise not to put Wentworth into debtor's prison should he come to London, together they worked out an elaborate scheme for settling the Wentworth debts. Briefly, it was that if the group could persuade the Crown to formally separate New Hampshire and Massachusetts and make New Hampshire a separate colony with Wentworth as the first Royal Governor, then he could make enough money out of the office to repay his debts.

It worked. New Hampshire was given the edge in the Massachusetts-New Hampshire border dispute (the line still holds) and in spite of the protest of many irate people in both New Hampshire and Massachusetts, Benning Wentworth became New Hampshire's first Royal Governor with a commission from George II. He dropped his claim against the British government and assumed his own debts. And so he was inaugurated on January 14, 1741, instead of languishing in debtor's prison.

Governor Wentworth soon made pots of money, mostly in land speculation in Vermont, but first he got the Assembly to give him a permanent salary, an innovative idea in those days. Clearly he meant to control and rule like a king over the 20,000 inhabitants of New Hampshire whose western border he declared to be 20 miles east of the Hudson. He made Portsmouth into a snobbish capital dominated by wealthy merchants and the Episcopal church, which was headed by the Rev. Arthur Browne, whose daughter married Robert Rogers of the Rangers. He cultivated the arts when he became rich, giving money to Harvard to rebuild the burned library and land to Dartmouth for its first buildings.

A most intriguing tale about pompous, fat, rich, and flamboyant Benning Wentworth is told by Henry W. Longfellow in a long narrative poem, "Lady Wentworth." On his sixtieth birthday Wentworth, now a widower, lived in lonely splendor in his mansion, which is still standing in Portsmouth. He invited a large party for dinner and had the Rev. Arthur Browne sitting by his side.

After dinner the host called for silence and motioned to a servant. Into the room was ushered a beautiful 20-year-old serving maid, Martha Hilton, who had worked as a housemaid in the mansion for five years. Martha was dressed in the latest style, her hair curled and her manner demure. The Governor rose and took her by the hand and presented her to the company as his prospective wife. The whisper of excitement that swept the hall was hushed when the Governor turned to the minister and asked him to perform the ceremony on the spot. He did.

Mr. and Mrs. Benning Wentworth lived happily ever after as far as history records. He retired as governor in 1766 and died ten years later, a controversial man all his life, a man to build legends on.

21. Cadwallader Colden and the New York Claims — 1760-1776

Governor Benning Wentworth had a foe over in New York Colony who also had a powerful influence on Vermont and a life worth recalling, Lt. Gov. Cadwallader Colden. Born in Scotland in 1688, he came to America in 1708 after graduating at the University of Edinburgh. He was trained as a doctor, but his writings, which were many, were mostly on astronomy and botany. He became surveyor general of New York Colony, held various political jobs, and in the meantime published a history of the Indians and a learned treatise on the diseases in America. He founded the American Philosophical Society.

An intense and scholarly man, not seeking personal riches,

he retired to his home in Newburgh, New York, in 1760, but was soon appointed lieutenant governor of New York, an office he held until his death in 1776. He made himself violently unpopular trying to enforce the Stamp Act, but he chiefly concerns Vermonters because of his widely publicized quarrels with Benning Wentworth over the New Hampshire grants.

The New York claim to the Vermont area was based on the grant made by Charles II to the Duke of York in 1664, which included "all the Land from the West side of the Connecticut River to the East Side of Delaware Bay." New Hampshire's claim was that since Massachusetts and Connecticut had extended their western boundary to 20 miles east of the Hudson, they would too. Also, Wentworth produced a copy of his commission as governor which indicated that the western boundary of New Hampshire extended west "till it meets with other governments."

New York officials didn't seem to get particularly excited about the New Hampshire claims until Colden came on the scene as lieutenant governor. Not all the New York Council members approved of Colden's claim, but complaints were taken to the King by both sides in 1763, by which time Wentworth had granted over a hundred towns in Vermont.

Colden, then acting governor, issued a proclamation "commanding and requiring all judges, justices, and civil officers within [New York Province] to continue to exercise their respective functions as far as the banks of the Connecticut River ... notwithstanding contrariety of jurisdiction claimed by the government of New Hampshire."

The mostly poor, rugged, energetic, and adventurous people who had staked their labor and money on an agreement with New Hampshire did not take kindly to the idea that their grants were invalid and that they would have to get out or pay a second purchase price to New York for the land. Since there were no local newpapers, it was word of mouth that carried the news through backwoods settlements, inciting anger that swept like fire in dry leaves. The stage was set for a hot fight.

22. Land Grants — 1749-70

The story of the land grants in the disputed area that would become Vermont is so complex that a chronological summary is needed to fix the facts in mind.

From 1749 to 1764 Governor Wentworth granted about three million acres in 138 towns in the New Hampshire Grants, as the territory came to be known. After years of apathy to New Hampshire's grants, New York, stirred by Lt. Gov. Colden, woke up and became howling mad at Benning Wentworth's scheme and sent emissaries to the King, who in 1764 announced that New York was right, that her boundary went to the western bank of the Connecticut River. Furthermore, New York construed this to mean that the New Hampshire grants were nullified, accordingly divided the Grants into three counties, and set up county officers.

It is important to remember the political attitude of the settlers. New Hampshire, like the rest of New England, regarded the townships as little republics in which the people at town meetings appointed their own officers. The inhabitants of the Grants were enraged at the centralized government dictated by New York, a colony founded on feudal ideas with large land holdings, manor houses and a class society. The Grants were as classless as a society could be, each man's measure taken by the amount of physical work he could do.

New York then entered into a vigorous campaign to collect quitrents, a confirmatory fee that all New Hampshire grantees were ordered to pay to New York. The tax seems very small even by the standards of the day, but a principle was involved as well. The settlers had paid for the lands to a representative of the Crown, and most of them boiled, balked, and refused to pay. To make matters worse, New York then began to issue land grants herself, sometimes on land already under cultivation. By 1765 New York survey teams began to show up around Bennington, causing more outrage.

If one side could appeal to the King, so could the other. Over

600 Wentworth proprietors sent a petition to King George III by agent Samuel Robinson of Bennington. The King took it to heart and advised New York in 1767 not to issue any more charters and not to press any more quitrents until the problem could be studied. "Studies" in those days were no faster than they are today, so this was just the cooling-off period the settlers needed. They relaxed and hoped the matter was settled.

But not for long, for New York was simmering. Thinking, probably quite rightly, that nothing would come of the study, they took the initiative in 1769, and Colden issued 600,000 more acres in New York patents, mostly to a handful of wealthy Yorkers, one of whom was a man cordially hated in the Grants, lawyer James Duane.

Some of the Wentworth grantees bowed to New York and paid the quitrent, but most said they'd rather die than pay, along with a number of unprintable remarks. Farmers armed themselves — those who could afford the arms — and prepared to fight it out with the survey teams that were rumored to be on the way.

It was not an idle rumor. A survey team arrived at the farm of James Breakenridge of Bennington. The story goes that about 60 of his neighbors were assisting in harvesting his corn, so the assembled group ceased harvesting and turned to defense and ran the surveyors away. Contemporary points of view describe this as anything from a peaceful parley to a violent riot. At any rate the affair precipitated a series of ejectment suits by Yorkers, and soon a number of them were scheduled for the Supreme Court at Albany. Something had to be done about this, legally and soon.

In the winter and spring of 1770 some Connecticut proprietors came forward to assist the nine farmers whose cases were to be taken to court. An emergency fund was raised by settlers and their friends. But they needed a person to head this loose organization, a person who could command the trust and authority that would be vested in him.

And this is how the man and moment met. Ethan Allen was just such a person.

23. *Ethan Allen Enters* — *1737-1770*

Ethan Allen, man and myth, has been a controversial figure for historians. Books pro, books con, old newpaper articles, and Allen's writings themselves all show many sides of him, as is proper for a folk hero. For folk hero he is.

Ethan Allen was born in Litchfield, Connecticut, on January 10, 1737, old style, or January 21 by today's calendar. (Colonial records were greatly confused by the eighteenth century change by England from the Julian to the Gregorian calendar. England was long overdue; the rest of Europe had changed in the sixteenth century by edict of Pope Gregory, the ancient church calendar being found in error.)

When Ethan was two, his father sold his farm and moved his family to Cornwall, a raw little frontier community harassed by Indians and wild animals. Ethan's parents, Joseph and Mary Baker Allen, were equal to the hardships, however. They produced (after the birth of the eldest son Ethan) Heman, Lydia, Heber, Levi, Lucy, Zimri, and Ira. All the boys grew to maturity, a rare thing indeed in that day and place. Like his father, Ethan was strong and energetic, accustomed to hard work and physical rigor.

His schooling was fragmentary, but he learned to read from his parents and spent hours revelling in the Old Testament and *Plutarch's Lives*. He aspired to go to Yale, so his father, encouraging his intellectual bent, arranged to have the boy tutored by the Congregational minister, the Rev. Jonathan Lee, in nearby Salisbury. Within a few months Ethan was called home. His father had died, leaving the responsibility of the family squarely on the eldest son.

Joseph Allen had left his family well-fixed with land and a going farm, yet someone had to run it. Ethan's dreams of college vanished, but he did not lose his intellectual zeal in the unremitting work of farming. Somehow he kept his spirit of curiosity in the world around him, and all his life he would think of himself first as a man of letters.

When Ethan was 19, Connecticut men were mustered to fight Montcalm, who was marching with his French army against Fort William Henry on Lake George, New York. Ethan reported for duty, no doubt excited about the venture from home. The Connecticut company got as far as what is now southern Vermont when word came that it was too late. The fort had fallen to the French. Two weeks later Ethan found himself home again with the shovel and hoe while the musket went back to the mantel rack. The French and Indian wars were almost over, and Ethan's vigor was not needed for the conflict that had occupied the colonies for the past four generations.

In 1762 Ethan became part owner of an iron business in Salisbury, and the same year he took a wife, Mary Brownson. By some accounts she was a miserable prize, older than Ethan, sharp tongued, plain, and whining. It has been suggested that Ethan, pressed for money in his new business, liked the bank account of the daughter of the prosperous miller, but that is idle speculation.

History does indicate, however, that he was an inattentive husband at best. Poor Mary Allen probably had reason to complain and make shrewish remarks, for she was sadly neglected all their 20 years of marriage. She could not read or write, which must have been frustrating to her and mortifying to Ethan, a man who took pride in his literary bent.

They had five children to whom Ethan appears to have been an indifferent father, for he was seldom at home. He would go away for weeks at a time to investigate the Grants and to visit his friends who had moved up into the new territory around Bennington. Ethan had seen this land when he was a lad going off to fight. The memory of it had lingered, but he had made no purchases, although he made the rounds of the taverns as often as he could leave Salisbury.

Soon after his marriage, Ethan Allen turned over the family farm to his younger brothers and bought one for himself near his iron works in Salisbury. The iron works eventually became a success thanks probably to Ethan's enthusiasm for whatever he undertook. But money was tight, and in 1764 he sold part of his share in the business to his brother Heman, who had moved to Salisbury to work for Ethan.

Heman evidently had the same kind of joy of living that possessed Ethan. The two Allen "boys" were always in trouble with the law for rather appealing sins, such as penning up the neighbor's pigs that had been a nuisance to the Allens, and the subsequent legal harassment of the neighbor in question. And Ethan, out at night rather than at home with Mary and the baby, was haled into court for brawling. These stories were told and enlarged upon in the taverns of the frontier area. Ethan was everbody's favorite as the subject of a good tale. Disturbing the peace was his talent.

One of Ethan's misdemeanors was that he illegally inoculated himself with smallpox serum as he felt that the Connecticut law forbidding it was foolish. Inoculations were at last beginning to catch on in America, thanks to Dr. Zabdiel Boylston who had introduced it in Boston in 1721. Inoculations had been successful on the eastern seaboard, but the practice was still regarded as witchcraft in the backwoods.

Even more entertaining was his arrest for blasphemy. Folk tales of Ethan's ability to swear still linger in the Green Mountains, and when he became drunk and disorderly he shocked the proper citizens. And Ethan liked to talk. Nothing was more exciting for him, or his listeners, than to sit for hours in a tavern with a bowl of grog and a good conversational partner. Such a friend was Dr. Thomas Young of Salisbury, a learned man, not much older than Ethan, who could converse on philosophy, medicine, politics, and natural wonders. But the field they most explored together was religion.

Ethan had been born an Episcopalian, his father being a free thinking man who did not hold with the Calvinist doctrines of hell and damnation. The doctrines of the Deists were discussed in intellectual circles in those days, thought that was basically contrary to Puritan religion. They believed in the existence of God on the evidence of nature and reason, and supernaturalism was not part of it. Ethan, like the Deists, believed that God had set the world in motion and would not interfere with the cosmic plan. Although the settlers in the Grants were never a churchy lot in the sense that the Plymouth colony had been, Ethan's thinking was still sufficiently heretical to produce some shock waves.

In the year 1763 Ethan and Young sat night after night in the tavern at Salisbury while 25-year-old Ethan and his friend hashed out the improbabilities of the Bible. Most of the philosophical learning came from Young, but Ethan had a great knowledge of the Bible and a faculty of observation of the world about him that brought the minds together as equals. They decided to write a book on religion, a book to tear down existing beliefs, and began to get the ideas on paper; but Dr. Young moved away from the area a year later before it was completed.

Ethan never saw his friend again, but long after Young's death Ethan was able to get the manuscript, add and edit and have the book published under his own name in 1785 when he was no longer a young man. Called *The Oracles of Reason*, it was published by the new firm of Haswell and Russel in Bennington, but Ethan had to agree to pay for the printing as it progressed. Haswell had learned his trade and business practices from the master of publishing, Isaiah Thomas, and could probably recognize a money-loser when he saw it.

Called popularly "Allen's Bible," the book was widely discussed but it did not sell well. It was attacked by the clergy and sneered at by some intellectuals, but nevertheless it was pure Allen and a remarkable book for its time.

24. Trials at Albany — 1770

Ethan had left Salisbury after selling his interest in the iron works and had moved to Northampton, Massachusetts, with his family. For reasons not recorded he was ordered to leave, and from there he went back to Salisbury and then to Sheffield, Massachusetts, but most of his time was spent hunting and fishing and visiting relatives in the Grants.

In 1770, when Ethan was 30 and the Grants dispute had reached a new high, he was chosen by a citizens' group in Bennington to go to Portsmouth, New Hampshire, to see Gov. John Wentworth, the nephew of old Gov. Benning Wentworth. Ethan was delighted to make the 150 mile trip through rugged wilderness to get the original land certificates and other papers that certified the New Hampshire land grants.

These papers would be taken as evidence to the forthcoming trial in Albany of the nine disputed homesteads. The present New Hampshire governor declined to offer any help other than to give Ethan the papers. He had suffered a stiff rebuke from the Crown for advising the grantees not to pay the New York quitrents, so he did not care to get involved in his neighbors' struggle. But he did advise Ethan Allen to employ the best lawyer available, Jared Ingersoll of New Haven, Connecticut. Money had been raised by interested persons in Connecticut to help the injured landowners, so the fee was assured.

Ethan, enchanted with his new job of arranger, went to Connecticut to get the help of native-born Ingersoll, a judge of the admiralty. A Yale graduate, he had been agent for the Connecticut Colony as well as holding the unpopular job of stamp agent. He was a noted lawyer, and his fee was doubtless as high as his prestige.

When the trials opened in Albany in June, 1770, Ethan had travelled over 400 miles for the Grants' cause and had become a local property owner himself, although his family was still in Massachusetts. He had recently bought land in Poultney and Castleton, about 1,000 acres in all, not quite as much as he owned in Connecticut.

The land granted by New York seems to have been totally speculative, with acreage placed in the hands of a few influential men who could get rich in a hurry from it. Among the owners were Lieutenant Governor Colden and Attorney James Duane, who would eventually claim 110 square miles of Grants land. Even the presiding judge, Robert Livingston, held title to New York land patents.

The first case, *Small vs. Carpenter*, not in itself a big one, was decisive for the entire New Hampshire Grants. One Isaiah Carpenter had procured a farm from New Hampshire in 1765 at Shaftsbury, near Bennington, and had settled there and farmed it. In 1769 Lieutenant Governor Colden granted the same land to Major John Small. Soldiers who had served in the colonial wars were granted considerable land in this area. Small tried to take possession, but he had mis-judged the temper of the Bennington crowd.

As soon as the Albany trial opened the judge upheld an objection by Duane, Small's lawyer, that the certificates of the Wentworth claims were not admissable as evidence. Since these titles were the basis for the defense, Ingersoll and Allen walked angrily out of the court announcing that it was prejudiced. The other eight suits whose defense was the same went uncontested.

Ingersoll returned to New Haven, but Ethan, putting up at the local tavern, was stopped before he left for Bennington by James Duane and his friends Mr. Banyer and John Tabor Kempe, attorney general of New York. They wanted to suggest, delicately, that it would be worth the while of Ethan Allen to persuade his Bennington friends to go along with the court decision and not to resist the mighty men of New York. He would be rewarded with money or land or whatever he asked.

Later, Duane insisted that he actually bribed Ethan, but Allen says he left the crooked trio with the stern warning that "The Gods of the Hills are not the Gods of the Valley."

The legal battle was over — but the fight had hardly begun. New York would eventually find out what Ethan's cryptic words meant.

25. The Green Mountain Boys Are Organized — 1770

As soon as Ethan Allen got back from the rigged trials at Albany in the summer of 1770, a group of citizens who had by then named themselves the Committee of Safety met to decide what must be done next. The decision was that Ethan would head a military organization of volunteers who would keep the Yorkers out by force by administering a frontier type of justice. When acting Governor Colden of New York heard the news he declared he would drive this mob back into the Green Mountains, upon which pronouncement Allen and the others declared themselves to be the Green Mountain Boys.

By the end of the summer they had branched out into several local companies with leaders chosen from the various towns. Among the leaders were Ethan's cousins Remember Baker and Seth Warner, whose names loom large in Vermont history. Headquarters for the Green Mountain Boys were at Fay's Tavern at the sign of the catamount in Bennington, and Ethan Allen was called the colonel commandant.

Ethan was a giant of a man, so strong that stories of his physical prowess still abound. His endurance was legendary and his reputation for drinking any man under the table was probably not exaggerated.

The Green Mountain Boys did not wear uniforms, but a sprig of evergreen in the hat band distinguished them. Ethan carried a sword and was reputed to have had some epaulettes of fancy gold braid to point him out as leader of the minuteman organization. No likeness of Ethan was ever painted in his lifetime, so all pictures and statues of him are from the imagination.

The population of the Grants was so small that the Green Mountain Boys needed popular support in the neighboring colonies to survive. More important, help from the king was needed. From 1770 to 1775 five petitions were drawn up by the

Grants people and sent to England. After all, they had done very well with Samuel Robinson's agency to England in 1767. But things moved more slowly now, and the petitions were largely ineffective.

The *Connecticut Courant* at Hartford was the newspaper most circulated around Bennington since the Grants had no newspaper. Ethan, who had always liked to write, sent many columns of protest about New York's high-handed actions to the Connecticut paper. He also printed pamphlets, as was the custom of the day. Many of his articles were not signed with his real name, but, again according to the custom of the time, used ringing pseudonyms. The Connecticut and Massachusetts citizens were solidly sympathetic toward the Grants' case.

The Green Mountain Boys were proud that they never killed a single person in their war with New York, but they did exercise some bizarre punishments. They used banishment, fists, clubs, and switching with a birch whip on miscreants from over the New York line.

If New York had immediately brought a great force against the angry upstart settlers, she could have put them down very quickly, but New York was afraid of the Crown. Also, Colden was replaced by a new governor, John Murray, Earl of Dunmore, an avaricious Scotsman who wanted to bleed money from the grantees in the easiest way. He simply continued to grant lands in the name of New York to those who were willing to gamble, to the tune of a half a million acres, mainly on lands already under Wentworth grants. Murray lasted only about a year and was replaced by Gov. William Tryon.

While New York changed governors the Green Mountain Boys had time to organize themselves into an efficient unit. By 1772 they had drawn up some firm rules: surveyors were not to be allowed in the Grants; no Yorker could remove any person from the Grants without the permission of the Committee of Safety in Bennington or the Green Mountain Boys. They agreed not to hinder New York judges or sheriffs or officials in the line of duty, but no grantee could accept confirmation from New York on pain of risking "the great displeasure of the Green Mountain Boys."

For five years, until 1775, they played a delaying game of harassment with New York until the American Revolution produced some strange political bedfellows.

26. Leading Green Mountain Boys

History is about people and what they did and their effect on each other and on the prevailing situation. Here are some of the early leaders who have a bearing on the development of Vermont.

Other than Ethan Allen, his brother Ira was probably the most influential man of his time in the Grants. Ira, the youngest of the eight Allen children of whom Ethan was the eldest, was born in Cornwall, Connecticut, in 1751 when Ethan was 14. He received a much better education than the latter, and he was able to set himself up as a surveyor at a young age. With the help of his older brothers he was a land-owner by the time he was 21. He was a writer too, and, among other documents, he wrote *History of the State of Vermont* which is still read widely today. His style is more clear and concise than the flowery prose of Ethan, who was forever plagued with the lack of formal education.

Ira was a lieutenant in his cousin Seth Warner's regiment of Green Mountain Boys. When Vermont began to undergo her shaky beginnings of independence it was Ira, more than Ethan, who played the leading part. Later, Ira emerges as the diplomat, the fixer, and the agent for the complexities of statehood.

A Green Mountain Boy whose colorful story lingers on is Remember Baker. Born in Connecticut in 1737, six years before Ethan, Baker served in the French and Indian War. During his journey through Vermont to Lake George, where he fought, he noted the fertile land and became an early settler of Arlington, where he built a grist mill, arriving there with a New Hampshire grant in 1764. A popular man, Remember Baker had been on his land for eight years when Yorker sheriff John Munro tried to kidnap him from his home, a story which we shall hear more of later. At 39 Baker was killed by the Indians in the summer following the capture of Fort Ticonderoga, in which he took part.

Robert Cochran was another Green Mountain Boy who left his mark. He came to Bennington from Massachusetts in 1768. Short, sharp, and tough, he was associated with the Green Mountain Boys from the start, and he was feared by the Yorkers. It was Cochran, along with Ethan and Remember Baker, who signed a flippant and funny reward notice for James Duane and John Kempe of New York after a price had been put on the heads of Allen, Baker, and Cochran. One imagines that this handwritten document which is still in existence in the Vermont Archives was drawn up over a bowl of grog at Fay's Tavern. Cochran served with distinction in the American Revolution, lived to be 74, and was buried in New York among his one-time enemies.

Dr. Jonas Fay, a man important to the future state of Vermont, came to Bennington with his father Stephen and his brother Joseph in 1766. Jonas Fay, six years senior to Ethan Allen, fought in the French and Indian War as a teenager. Later he would serve with Ethan at Ticonderoga and as a surgeon in Col. Seth Warner's regiment in the Revolution. The Fay family was central to the Green Mountain Boys and to political matters of the day, for it was at Fay's Tavern in Bennington, with its famous snarling catamount facing New York, that the organizing of Green Mountain Boys and much political maneuvering took place.

Seth Warner, head of the Bennington division of the Green Mountain Boys, deserves a larger place in Vermont history than he has been accorded. He came to Bennington from Connecticut in 1765 when he was 22 years old. Historian Hiland Hall says he was "uniformly successful in whatever he undertook." Later, Warner emerges as a great soldier in the Revolution. A big man physically, an intelligent man whose judgment was respected, "His manners were simple, natural and in all respects entirely free from any kind of affectation." He died at the age of 42 destitute, leaving an impoverished family.

Other leaders whose names appear again and again are Peleg Sunderland, Samuel Robinson, Isaac Tichenor, and Thomas Chittenden, whose star began to rise in the Grants when he arrived in 1773.

27. Trouble at Breakenridge Farm — 1771

James Breakenridge, whose name appears in old records under various spellings, owned a farm which lay directly on the 20 mile line, a border that New Hampshire claimed for her western boundary. Breakenridge was a central character in the New York Grants war, for war it was.

Of Scotch-Irish descent, Breakenridge had come among the earliest settlers to the Grants. He was one of the parties in the ejectment suits that Ethan had helped defend. Mr. Breakenridge was listed as a "rioter" by New York, as were most of his neighbors. In 1771 he was sent to England as an agent for the Grants with one of the five petitions that were drawn up in the area — but not much came of that.

After the first attempt to eject Breakenridge in 1769, he tried to keep on farming; this was just before the Green Mountain Boys took over. The 1769 affair was significant because it was the first overt act of violence and resistance in the dispute. New York had decided to make a test case of this tract of land, and on October 19, 1769, a group of Yorkers came over the line with a writ of ejectment for Breakenridge. Surveyors came along with their tools as well, but word had preceded them. About 60 men (the number varies) were gathered on the farm allegedly to help harvest corn.

Justice of the Peace Munro advanced and "read the riot act," literally. No violence took place but the temper was there. Munro reported the affair in full to Lieutenant Governor Colden who then issued a proclamation naming "the principal authors and actors in the riot." Breakenridge, the local minister Jedediah Dewey, Samuel Robinson, Nathaniel Holmes, Henry Waldridge, and Moses Robinson were all indicted as rioters but were never brought to trial. But that was not the end of the troubles. A few months later Munro made a second attempt to eject Mr. Breakenridge. All the listed rioters were subjected to harassment of this sort, but by this time the Green Mountain Boys were becoming established and they took over the defense of the border farms. By now settlers were not allowed to come to peaceful terms with the Yorkers even if they wanted to.

On the morning of July 18, 1771, when the crops were getting ripe and the weather was hot, a party of Yorkers estimated variously from 700 to 300, headed by Sheriff Henry Ten Eyck and Mayor Cuyler of Albany, could be seen coming. Mr. Breakenridge's house was again the goal. One hundred well armed Green Mountain Boys and their friends gathered. The house was barricaded with 18 men inside. A red flag was to be raised if help was needed.

The rest of the Green Mountain Boys hid themselves behind the hills that sheltered the road to the house, and the Breakenridge family was sent away for safety with neighbors. When the posse arrived they were stopped by six or seven men who allowed them to go forward to talk with Breakenridge. Then the hidden men put their hats on the tips of their muskets and raised them so they could be seen by the Yorkers who realized that they were in an ambush. When the intruders arrived at the house, Mr. Breakenridge informed them that the protection of the house was now in the hands of the town. There was much going back and forth, but Mr. Breakenridge would not give up. The sheriff's men grew fainthearted; many of them probably sympathized with the settlers. So the Yorkers retreated.

In musical comedy style this affair led to more persons being listed as rioters. To Ethan Allen's great regret he was not on hand, since he had gone to Poultney for a few days.

However, Remember Baker, Seth Warner, and Robert Cochran were there, and it was a great victory for the home team. Later Ethan wrote a pamphlet on the fray.

28. The Green Mountain Boys Strike — 1771

By early 1771 Ethan Allen had begun to buy land with his cousin Remember Baker and his brothers Ira, Hemen and Zimri, and other friends. They set up the Onion (Winooski) River Co. which eventually held 110 square miles of the choicest land in the Champlain region. Ethan has been accused of putting his politics where his purse was, but the fact is that Ethan owned no Grants land until after he had committed himself to the defense of the settlers.

At any rate, Ethan had a large stake in the territory as did most of the Green Mountain Boys, and their bizarre methods of property protection became legendary. They dressed themselves like Indians; they wore women's clothes; they blacked their faces. They terrified and teased and kept the Yorkers at bay. They accepted no adverse criticism.

One of the outspoken opponents of the Green Mountain Boys was Dr. Samuel Adams of Arlington. He had a New York title, settled before the land disputes began, and he was brazen enough to make rude remarks about the Green Mountain Boys. His friends warned him, but the doctor would not keep silent in his outrage at this frontier justice. So Adams was kidnapped and brought to Fay's Tavern. With Ethan presiding, the Bennington Committee of Safety held a trial and found him guilty of being a public nuisance.

For punishment they tied him in a chair and hoisted him to the height of the sign of the tavern, the stuffed catamount that kept his snarling face toward New York. For two hours the good doctor dangled safely 20 feet in the air while the citizens of the town had a good laugh. The doctor mended his ways.

In May 1771, William Cockburn, a New York surveyor, was

sent to a New York grant of land known as Socialborough, which included the New Hampshire grants of Rutland and Pittsford. There still exists a letter from Cockburn to James Duane, one of the proprietors of Socialborough. Writes Cockburn, "Your acquaintance Nathan (sic) Allen was in the woods with another party blacked and dressed like Indians."

Runners went to inform Cockburn that the Green Mountain Boys intended to kill him. Cockburn promised the band that he would leave at once and come no more and he departed on the Crown Point Road with all haste.

Samuel Gardenier bought a New York tract, and when he arrived to take over he found Ichabod Cross settled there with a New Hampshire title. They made a compromise, but that wasn't good enough for the Green Mountain Boys. Gardenier was driven out by a masked mob. Then Robert Cochran took care of some come-lately Yorkers at Poultney.

In October of 1771 Ethan learned that Yorkers were invading Rupert. He and Remember Baker and Robert Cochran and others swooped down on a group of Scotch Highlanders clearing land under New York titles. The Green Mountain Boys wiped out their possessions, burning the houses amidst much cursing. New York issued warrants for the Green Mountain Boys. Justice of the Peace John Munro declared he would get them to justice. In Albany Governor Tryon had an idea: why not offer a reward? And so the first of several rewards was issued, placing a price of 20 pounds on the heads of those who had ousted the Rupert settlers.

Said Ethan: "By Virtue of a late Law in the Province they are not allowed to hang any man until they have ketched him." The Green Mountain Boys took the reward notices as a big joke. Over a bowl of grog in Fay's Tavern, Ethan Allen, Remember Baker, and Robert Cochran replied to Governor Tryon by offering a 25 pound reward for James Duane and John Kempe, those New York lawyers. The people in the Grants howled with laughter and would not have harmed a Green Mountain Boy for any amount of money. Ethan posted his counter notices from the Grants to Connecticut and the Green Mountain Boys became even more celebrated.

29. Remember Baker and Yorker Warfare — 1772

In late March 1772, New York performed its most outrageous act yet. Sheriff Munro and a small band of Yorkers burst into the house of Remember Baker, Green Mountain Boy and "rioter," of Arlington. Baker and his wife and son were asleep. Rudely jarred by the noise of the intruders, Baker ran for his gun over the fireplace, but the assailants had taken it. He grabbed his axe and whacked the Yorkers as best he could, and, trusting that his family would not be harmed, chopped a hole in his roof and climbed out into the snow below.

But he was spotted, overpowered, and in the scuffle somebody cut off his thumb with a sword. Bleeding badly and poorly clothed he was tied into a sleigh and headed for Albany.

Meanwhile, Mrs. Baker slipped out and alarmed the neighbors. Remember Baker was kin to most of the people around there, and within an hour the Green Mountain Boys were gathered and riding. Halfway to Albany they overtook the posse and rescued Remember. All the sheriff's men fled but the indomitible Munro, who was captured and for some reason released. Baker was taken to the Catamount Tavern in Bennington, sewed up and returned home minus his thumb. Munro was the subject of keen harassment from that day on, for Baker was a popular fellow.

Remember's cousin Seth Warner went to Munro's house to get Baker's rifle. A fight ensued and Warner struck Munro with his sword, knocking him to the ground, after which he went in and got the rifle and rode away leaving Munro prone. This got Warner's name put on the "reward" list, and the town of Poultney voted him 100 acres of land for "vallor in cutting Esquire Munro, the Yorkite." The whole affair was well publicized in the Connecticut papers, and tempers were high.

A note on John Munro (there are various spellings of the name in old documents): he had gotten a military patent from

New York just inside the town of Shaftsbury, near Bennington, under the patronage of Duane and Kempe, and he acted as sheriff for New York. Someone called him a "bold, meddlin', person." Ira Allen recounts that he was eventually beaten up by the Green Mountain Boys and banished.

Although the Green Mountain Boys never took a life in all their skirmishes, they did plan to ambush and kill Governor Tryon of New York. The governor got wind of it and the plan failed, but word got around. Tryon invited the Fays to come to Albany to negotiate a peace, but Ethan Allen sent along a rude letter which ruined any chance of settlement. Ethan's enemies said that the Allens wanted to fight with New York, for the Allens had by now become large land holders. Ethan and Remember had gone to White Plains disguised as British officers and bought up a number of New Hampshire Grants, some of which they resold to Thomas Chittenden, who would one day become governor of Vermont.

The Green Mountain Boys were busy these days. Word came that the same Scotsman Reid who had been driven out of Rupert was back, this time near Otter Creek with some settlers who were ignorant of the land feud. The Green Mountain Boys drove them out in a fury, destroying everything. Then generous Ethan turned around and offered them some land of his free of charge.

And so the warfare went. Benjamin Spencer, a Yorker of Clarendon, was broken in on and abused; haystacks and houses were burned; persons were whipped and given "beech seal certificates" of welts on the backside. One Rev. Benjamin Hough was imprisoned for a few days, given a lashing, and exiled from the Grants.

On the other side, the Yorkers continued their mean behavior. Andrew Graham, a Scotsman who had spent seven years opening up 40 acres in Windham County, was driven out by a gang of Yorkers.

In 1774 Governor Tryon increased the rewards for the ringleaders of the Green Mountain Boys. Ethan declared this to be the "bloody acts," but about this time, according to brother Ira, Ethan boldly went to Albany, in effect thumbing his nose at the governor's reward.

But the time for such tricks was over. A larger matter was on the horizon, promulgated by a man named Philip Skene.

30. A New Colony? — 1774

Ira Allen's history of Vermont which gives an eyewitness account of the critical period of the Grants in the 1770's. One little known affair he recounts was the first attempt to turn the area into a separate political entity.

"In the year 1774," writes Allen, "to get rid of the colony of New York, a plan was formed by Colonel Allen, Mr. Amos Bird, and other principal characters among the people, in conjunction with Colonel Philip Skene, to have established a new royal colony, which was to contain the grants of New Hampshire, west of the Connecticut River, and the country north of the Mohawk River, to latitude 45 degrees north, and bounded west by Iroquois River and Lake Ontario. Colonel Skene had been an officer in his Majesty's service, and had retired on a large patent of land lying at the south end of Lake Champlain, which was called Skenesboro, a proper sscite (sic) for the capital of the new colony, of which he was proposed to be Governor."

"The honor and lucrative prospects thus presented to Colonel Skene, stimulated him to go to London at his own expence (sic), to solicit the accomplishment of an important object to individuals, and to the public: for had he succeeded, the people who had settled under the royal grants of New Hampshire would have been quiet, and relieved from the oppressive conduct of the Governor and Council of the colony of New York."

So Colonel Skene did go to London, and, by some string-pulling, got himself appointed governor of the garrisons of Ticonderoga and Crown Point. He had fought at the former with General Abercrombie in 1759. The new colony was to have Lake Champlain at its center. Colonel Skene had grandiose ideas in keeping with his 300,000 acres of land.

He had met Ethan Allen in about 1770 when Ethan was living in Poultney, near Skenesboro (now Whitehall), New York, and the two men had liked each other. Even after Ethan was outlawed and Skene was a justice of the peace for New York they continued the friendship. They agreed that the Grants should be a separate colony, the only point of difference being that Skene saw it as a larger province than did Ethan.

When Skene went to London in 1774 Ethan was in accord with the project. After Skene got royal approval he was to get a petition from the inhabitants, but the temper of the people was suddenly against anything smacking of a royal colony.

If Skene had initiated this move two years sooner he would no doubt have succeeded, as it was a perfect solution to the dispute between New York and the Grants. Our history might have been totally different.

But at this moment the colonies were uniting and the people were rising up to resist the Crown. The anger at the mother country was even hotter than the anger at New York, and Skene's plan fell through.

Vermont heard from Skene again, for he fought against the Americans at Bennington and at Castleton, and much later his partially implemented plan to make the Grants into a royal colony and his nebulous appointment as governor was to be a lever in the delicate negotiations for statehood.

Skene did another thing that was important to the settlement of Vermont. He cut a road at his own expense through the woods from Skenesboro to Salem in Washington County, New York, and later extended it to Bennington and to Williamstown, Massachusetts. This became the principal route for the colonization of northern Vermont. He also had sailing sloops on Lake Champlain, some of which were seized for Ethan Allen's use in the capture of Fort Ticonderoga.

Philip Skene's idea of making the Grants region into a royal colony laid the foundation for the Republic of Vermont which was just over the horizon.

31. Conventions and Tempers — 1774

Before there was central government in the Grants, the towns were run as small republics. New Hampshire made little effort to govern the region, but New York set it up into (subject to some changes along the way) three counties, Cumberland, Bennington, and Gloucester, with a shire town or county seat in each area where a court was held and justice administered. Most people, including the Green Mountain Boys, agreed to this loose government as long as their land titles were not disturbed. The royal order of 1764 had extended the jurisdiction of New York to the west bank of the Connecticut River.

But all was not peace in Cumberland County, which was roughly the present Windham and Windsor counties. As early as 1770 when the shire town was at Chester, Nathan Stone entered the court house, and claiming to act in public behalf, denied the New York right to hold the court. John Grout, a Chester lawyer, who openly sympathized with New York, was first taken prisoner, then forced out of town and prohibited from the practice of law.

In 1772 Westminster was made the county seat since the Chester atmosphere was too lawless to suit the court, but it too proved to be a lively spot.

As the fight with New York mushroomed, towns set up committees or councils of safety. The Bennington Council of Safety, whose records can still be read, was the best known of these. After a few years the committee realized that they should act together and hold some joint meetings, so they called a convention in Manchester in April 1774.

The Grants people were not entirely unified against New York. There was considerable "Tory" activity in Cumberland County — Tory activity in this sense meaning that they were New York sympathizers. But a third force was arising: the annoyance of the colonists with the government of Britain, especially over the matter of taxation.

In May 1774 a committe of correspondence from the Continental Congress that was to meet in the fall wrote the supervisors of Cumberland County to find out the sentiments of the people about the oppressive English laws. The persons who received the letter did not distribute it, but finally two Whigs, Dr. Reuben Jones of Rockingham and Capt. Azariah Wright of Westminster, found out about it and circulated the convention letter to the public.

A county convention was thereupon called to meet in Westminster on October 19, 1774. The people of Chester were consulted, and on October 10 five persons were chosen to attend the convention. They brought a resolution that showed the temper of the times: "That the people of America are naturally intitled to all the priviledges of free born subject of Great Britain (sic) . . . That all the acts of the British Parliament tending to take away or abridge these rights ought not to be obeyed . . . " This set the tone of the Westminster meeting the following week.

Meanwhile the Continental Congress had met in Philadelphia on September 5 and an agreement was made there that there would be no more commerce with the mother country until the obnoxious acts of Parliament were repealed and that there would be no more commerce with colonies which did not agree to this. New York was the only dissenter. The Grants people had no representation at the Continental Congress other than the nebulous connections with New York and New Hampshire.

The Cumberland County group met peaceably for two balmy October days, and Col. John Hazeltine of Townshend was chosen chairman. Despite grievances with the Crown they declared loyalty to it, but at the same time supported the acts of the Continental Congress.

Lt. Leonard Spaulding of Dummerston was arrested by New York authorities on October 28, 1774, for calling the king "the pope of Canada" and was jailed at Westminster. Spaulding was vociferously angry about the Quebec Act, as were a lot of other people who felt the terms were too lenient to the French "habitants." After all, New Englanders had fought the French in Canada for a long time, and they were annoyed that the British government had turned around and allowed the former French citizens to remain Catholic and to have some share in the government. From today's perspective it appears that British statesmen were trying to behave in an enlightened and humane manner, but the recent veterans of the French wars did not see it that way.

Spaulding's friends from Dummerston gathered up a crowd of angry sympathizers from adjoining towns, broke into the jail, and liberated Spaulding. Fury was in the air.

Col. Hazeltine on November 13 then called a second meeting at Westminster for November 30. Twenty-one towns were represented. Opposition to the colonial laws of England was again aired. But it was at the third meeting in Westminster the following March that violence erupted, and Grants people emerged with a real rallying point that led to independence.

32. The Stage is Set for Trouble — 1775

Cumberland County Court was to meet on March 14, 1775, at Westminster. Mutters and grumbles had abounded in the eastern section of the Grants that the courts, which were run by New York, were unfair and used oppressive force against the Grants people. Up to this point, the focus of discord against New York had been in Bennington. The people of Cumberland, the eastern county, were more friendly to New York. Ethan Allen had hoped that something would make the Cumberland people unite with the western Grants people for a massive resistance to New York tyranny. His wish was about to come true.

Matters had reached such a point in Cumberland County that citizens were earnestly seeking reform in the court. For one thing, the court met too often and called too many jurors. Four times a year over 70 farmers were called for jury duty, an outrageous inconvenience for working farmers in a poorly populated area. They had long rough roads to travel to the county seat in all kinds of weather, and they were not properly compensated for their time.

In February 1775 citizens gathered at Westminster to discuss their grievances and to present a plan for improvement which included holding only two courts a year, with fewer jurors. Power was invested in the chairman of the committee, Col. Hazeltine, to call meetings, and a committee was chosen to keep the friends of liberty from other towns in touch. The minutes were ordered published so that the people would know that the committee supported the Continental Congress, which had met the previous September, especially in the matters of non-importation and non-commerce and in objections to the court system.

Along with the indignation against New York there was an increasing resentment against the mother country. In Dummerston a gun had been taken away forcibly from a noted Tory who had spoken out against the Continental Congress. So it was evident that there were two forces stirring the people: anger at New York court practices and anger at the taxation policies of England.

The Whigs who were dissenting from the establishment began to be known as "the Mob" and the conservative Tories were called "the Court Party." With the division between the two groups growing wider all the time, thoughtful men in the area feared that violence would result.

So, wrote eyewitness Dr. Reuben Jones of the later eruption, "[on March 10] Accordingly there were about 40 good and true men went from Rockingham to Chester to dissuade Col. Chandler, the chief judge, from attending court. He said he believed that it would be for the good of the county not to have court as things were; but there was one case of murder that they must see to, and if that was not agreeable to the people they would not have any other case."

One of the 40 good men reminded the judge that the rumor was going around that the Yorker Sheriff William Paterson was out rallying the Tories to come with firearms, but Judge Chandler gave his word that no arms would be brought against the Whig group. The judge further said that he would

67

go to the court a day early to keep peace, and they parted on friendly terms.

Judge Chandler was a respected man despite his politics. Later, when he was jailed for political reasons, he was well treated and released promptly. In time he became a patriotic supporter of the emerging United States, but his early connection with the New York court was always held against him by some people. Years later the poor fellow died in debtor's prison, although he had been pardoned by a legislative act that came too late. He was buried, with no funeral service or marker, outside the wall of the old cemetery in Westminster because he had died in prison.

Sheriff Paterson, on the other hand, was held highly to blame in the troubles to come. He languished in the Northampton jail for a long time and nobody had a good word for him.

33. The Westminster Massacre — 1775

In Westminster court day was approaching and trouble was in the March air. According to Dr. Reuben Jones, "there was a great deal of talk in what manner to stop the court; and at length it was agreed on to let the court come together, and lay the reasons we had against their proceedings, before them, thinking they were men of such sense that they would hear them. But on Friday we heard that the court was going to take possession of the house on the 13th inst., and to keep a strong guard at the doors of said house, that we could not come in."

And so "the Mob," as the protestors were called, decided to beat them to it, and on Monday, March 13, about a hundred Whigs entered and occupied the court house at about four in the afternoon, armed with staves picked up from Capt. Azariah Wright's woodpile, as most of them were too poor to own firearms. It was mud season, and probably the hundred men were fired by that special Vermont March spring fever as well as anger at the court and Crown.

Dr. Jones goes on to say: "But we had but just entered, before we were alarmed by a large number of men, armed with guns, swords, and pistols. But we, in the house, had not any weapons of war among us, and we were determined that they should not come in with their weapons of war, except by the force of them."

Sheriff Paterson came up at the head of his Tory followers and commanded the Mob to disperse. No answer. Heads looked out the windows, and everybody stood still to hear the hated sheriff read the king's proclamation for court and to tell those inside that if they did not disperse in 15 minutes that he would "blow a lane through them." The Mob replied that they would not disperse. Tradition suggests in what inelegant terms they phrased their replies, but the language is not reported in the official account. The Mob leader said that the sheriff's men could enter if they unarmed themselves, but they declined that offer. Instead, they agreed to hold a parley.

At that, Samuel Gale, the clerk of the court, drew a pistol, held it up, and said, (sic) "D--n the parley with such d----d rascals, but by this — holding up the pistol. They gave us very harsh language, told us we should be in hell before morning."

The sheriff and his men withdrew to confer, and three of the mob went out to discuss the matter, but the sheriff's men would not talk to them.

At about five in the afternoon Judge Chandler came to the court house and told them that the armed men had come without his knowledge and that the Mob could stay in the court house until morning, and that there would be no arms at the court. At this promise, some of the occupants went home to friends or lodgings for the night leaving a sentry and a watch party within the court house. The sheriff's men dispersed, and things seemed to be calming down properly.

At about midnight matters picked up. The sheriff's men had been at Norton's Tavern, the Tory headquarters, and they were full of grog and bravado. The sentry at the court house saw them coming, Sheriff Paterson strutting in front of his band of Tories, and gave the word to man the doors and windows. The people in the court house were alert and sober since they had had no chance to slip a flip at a tavern. With only the light of a few torches to see by, the Mob saw the attackers stop about ten rods from the door. They listened with horrified disbelief as Paterson, with no discussion, no warning, gave the word to fire.

"Three fired immediately. The word fire was repeated; God D--m you fire, send them to hell, was most or all the words that were to be heard from some time: on which there were several men wounded."

The sheriff's forces rushed in with swords and clubs and beat up the outnumbered Whigs in the building. Then they pushed those who did not escape into the jail which was in the same building, dragging in the wounded with most inhuman behavior.

Young William French had four bullets in his body and died before morning. The 22-year-old son of Nathaniel French had lived in Brattleboro near the Dummerston line and was esteemed as "a clever, steady, honest, working farmer." It was reported that the sheriff's party brutalized the dying man and hurled curses onto his body; such conduct polarized the feeling in the Grants among previously neutral people.

Those who escaped the jail ran out to inform the people in the surrounding towns. Dr. Jones rode hatless to Dummerston to shout the news. On Tuesday morning the townspeople and the visitors to the court were stunned when they found the court house a bloody mess. By noon when 400 or so angry men from New Hampshire and the Grants had arrived armed with a variety of weapons, the first thing they did was to free the prisoners, for they had trudged through the March mud looking for a fight.

The wounded had been taken to nearby houses, chiefly that of Capt. Azariah Wright. Nine days later one of the wounded, Daniel Houghton of Dummerston, died of wounds he had received from the sheriff's party. He was cared for at the home of Eleazer Larlow and is buried at Westminster.

With the angry outsiders pouring in and blood still on the floor, court convened on Tuesday morning at the stated time. The benches were broken but the shaken judges sat down to prepare a statement of the affair. The document they produced presents a moderate view of the doings compared to Dr. Jones' heated deposition, but the same basic facts are there.

After a little while, with the air becoming more and more tense as more men arrived, the court was adjourned until three o'clock. It turned out to be a final adjournment, for the New York Court never met in the Grants again. For all practical purposes New York rule came to an end at that moment. The Mob took over, and the sheriff, the court officials, and all the Tories they could catch were penned up in the jail where the Whigs, now freed, had been lodged earlier. There was such a crowd in town that there were no more rooms and food supplies were low.

On Wednesday the inquest was held on the body of French who was buried later that day. His gravestone with the epitaph below still stands in the Westminster cemetery.

In Memory of WILLIAM FRENCH.
Son to Nathaniel French. Who Was Shot at Westminster March ye 13th, 1775. by the hands of Cruel Ministerial tools. of George ye 3rd, in the Courthouse at 11 a Clock at night in the 22d, year of his Age

Here WILLIAM FRENCH his Body lies.
For Murder his Blood for Vengance cries.
King George the third his Tory crew tha with a bawl his head Shot threw.
For Liberty and his Countrys Good.
he lost his Life his Dearest blood.

34. A Change of Focus — 1775

Robert Cochran with a party of Green Mountain Boys arrived in Westminster on March 15, 1775. Ethan Allen wasn't with them, but he sent word that he would come soon to help out. The 40 Green Mountain Boys were armed with swords and pistols, and their distinguishing green spruce twigs were stuck jauntily in their hat bands. Cochran tauntingly asked the jailed court party why they did not arrest him and collect the reward that was on his head.

The arrival of the West Side contingent which had for some years been battling the New York government gave a sense of unity that had never before existed in the Grants. The excited Mob wanted to burn down the court house and execute the court members, but level-headed leader Capt. Benjamin Bellows "did not forget what was due to justice." Captain Bellows, feeling that the prisoners should be punished in a legal manner, discouraged any retaliatory violence from the enraged Mob, and the people heeded his advice.

Elsewhere in town other exciting events were taking place. Leonard Spaulding, that colorful character from Dummerston who had been jailed (and released by his friends) for saying harsh words about George III, set up his own inspection service, capturing and interviewing all the sheriff's party that he could find. Dr. Solomon Harvey, heading 300 Whigs, captured and brought in four more of the escaping sheriff's posse.

There were several written accounts and much folklore stemming from the so-called massacre. Dr. Reuben Jones's version was probably the most correct. The "State of the Facts" had been drawn up by the court, and various newspaper accounts appeared later in Massachusetts, Connecticut and New York papers.

Dr. Jones was among the earliest and most ardent Whigs in Cumberland County. A stirrer-up of men, popular and energetic, he early saw the possibilities of the Grants as a separate state. He was a literate man who was often chosen for clerk at the many conventions he attended. There is no doubt that he was one of the leaders who brought the tempers of the people to the point of the massacre. Later he would go to Washington on behalf of Vermont, serve as surgeon in the Revolutionary War, and sit in the Legislature of the Republic of Vermont. In 1821 the Legislature voted to pay him $100 for his past services. Yet he, like many of the men of his period who worked hard for causes they believed in, died penniless after being released from debtor's prison by the influence of friends in his old age.

Benjamin Hall whose *History of Eastern Vermont*, written in 1858, contains much original material, says the term "massacre" is not correct. He believes that "insurrection" was the better word, since this was an uprising against injustice after peaceable means had failed.

In any case, in spite of the epitaph of William French, the uprising was against New York and not against the Crown as such. French's gravestone was erected just a few weeks after the affair at Westminster, after the Battle of Lexington which took place in April. The focus changed very quickly at that point, but no one denies that French was a victim in the fight for freedom.

On Sunday the court prisoners were taken to Northampton, Massachusetts, and jailed. Most of them were released quickly, but Sheriff Paterson was held for some months. Colonial justice was in shambles with the onset of the Revolution.

The alleged murderer for whom the court was called on March 14 is perhaps the one on whom the whole thing can be blamed, for the court would never have convened had it not been for this mysterious character and his crime!

35. The April Meeting at Westminster — 1775

With men still milling around Westminster, loath to go home, the leaders thought the mood should be captured. Probably engineered by Capt. Azariah Wright, Dr. Reuben Jones, and Robert Cochran of the Green Mountain Boys, the decision was made to hold a congress at Westminster on April 11, 1775, less than a month away. This seemed a fine idea and visitors went home to tell their neighbors to elect some delegates.

Ethan Allen, who had not been on hand for the massacre or its aftermath, hurried over from Bennington to make sure that he would have a chance to take part in the meeting, for at last here were his dreams come true: the possibility of a real union of the east and west sides of the Grants. Allen had privately said that he considered most of the easterners safety-conscious Tories, but now the eastern Grants' break with New York was as final as could be.

This April 11 meeting was especially significant because it was the first time, other than in Skene's personal vision and attempt, that the entire Grants had been viewed as a potential political entity.

Dr. Jones was appointed clerk and Major Abijah Lovejoy was chosen moderator. Several important resolutions were made to be addressed to the Crown: that the inhabitants were in danger of having their property taken from them by New York; that the lives of the people endangered as shown by the recent massacre; that "it was the duty of said inhabitants . . . to wholly renounce and resist the administration of the government of New York till such time as the lives and property of those inhabitants may be secured by it . . . with a humble petition, to be taken out of so oppressive a jurisdiction and, either annexed to some other government and incorporated into a new one, as may appear best to said inhabitants . . . " Finally they voted that Ethan Allen, John Hazeltine, and Charles Phelps, Esq., be a committee to prepare such a remonstrance.

This was the first clear indication of the will of the people to unite and withdraw from New York. It may be assumed that Ethan Allen was ecstatic; at last he had the support both of the eastern and the western Grants against New York, and he was selected to do what he liked best — to write protests.

Almost everybody in the Grants was happy about this turn of events, but the people of Guilford had assembled on March 28, 1775, and voted that they preferred the government of New York despite the massacre. That vote didn't hold up very long, however, for on April 7 the Guilford commissioners from New York were forced by irate neighbors to resign. A town fight developed which was settled before long in favor of the anti-Yorker crowd.

On April 19, 1775, over in Concord and Lexington, Massachusetts, another group of farmers was hiding behind bridges and trees to take shots at the British regulars who were out to get the powder stored in the neighborhood. This was considered the beginning of the American Revolution.

The Westminster Massacre, the April 11 convention at Westminster, and Battle of Lexington — all of which fell within little more than a month — forever fused the issues. The break with New York and the break with the mother country were never clearly separated in Vermont politics. And very soon these matters would become further involved with Vermont's next step — that of becoming an independent state.

36. Ethan Allen's Plan — 1775

After the April 11, 1775, convention at Westminster, Ethan Allen began writing the paper of remonstrance and grievances to the king, with the support of most of the people of the Grants behind him, but evidently he never completed it. By the time the news of the Battle of Lexington reached Bennington, a far more interesting project presented itself to Ethan.

Up on Lake Champlain Fort Ticonderoga stood reputedly filled with cannon and firearms and ammunition and guarded, it was said, by a mere handful of British regulars. With open hostilities now at hand there was every reason to believe that the British would reinforce the garrison and use it for a base of operations against the rebellious colonies. The British would then be in control of Lake Champlain and its adjacent waterways.

Ethan Allen, among other people, looked at the map and considered. Why not have the Green Mountain Boys seize the fort now, quickly, and use it for the Continental Army? He thought it over for a few days. True, the spirit of separation from the Crown seemed to have swept the colonies; then again, the king might quell the rebellion and a few insubordinate Green Mountain Boys would risk swinging from tall gallows if they had invaded His Majesty's fort.

But messengers coming from Connecticut and Massachusetts with newspapers, written messages, and word of mouth details from committees of correspondence brought the news that Boston was up in arms and that a patriot army was in the making. Ethan decided to act; he sent word to the Green Mountain Boys to gather in Castleton. Back in Connecticut, meanwhile, another part of the venture was forming.

Benedict Arnold had had the same idea about capturing Fort Ticonderoga. He was on his way to Boston with a company of Connecticut militia to offer help when he ran into Samuel Parsons, a member of the Hartford Committee of Correspondence. Arnold mentioned his thoughts about Fort Ticonderoga and continued on to Boston.

When Parsons got back home he called on some friends who were also on the Hartford committee. This self-appointed group of patriots decided to draw 300 pounds out of the Connecticut colonial treasury and finance an attack on Fort Ticonderoga. Within a few hours eight men were on their way to Bennington to raise troops and confer with Ethan Allen. They picked up 50 men en route in Massachusetts and sent word to Ethan who was already getting things moving up north. On May 2 they got together at Fay's Tavern in Bennington.

In the meantime, Noah Phelps from Connecticut had gone ahead to spy out the fort. Posing as a woodcutter, he wandered into the fort asking for a haircut. He saw at first hand how poorly the fort was defended and was able to report to Allen that the detachment there had not even heard the news of the Battle of Lexington.

By this time about 200 men were in Castleton. By late Sunday, May 7, the Connecticut and Massachusetts troops also reached Castleton. Ethan Allen was unanimously chosen commander of the expedition, and a committee of war was chosen by the leaders. It was decided that daybreak, May 10, would be the hour of assault on the fort.

Fort Ticonderoga had been originally called Fort Carillon when it was built by the French in 1755. General Amherst had captured it from them in 1759 and renamed it Fort Ticonderoga. After the French menace had subsided the fort was allowed to deteriorate, but now in 1775 it was to experience its most famous hour.

37. Benedict Arnold Arrives —1775

What was about to happen in the Lake Champlain area had a certain musical comedy element. Benedict Arnold, last seen on his way to defend Boston, appeared on the scene again.

Benedict Arnold did many things besides betray his country. He began life as a horse dealer and then he became a druggist and a bookseller in New Haven, Connecticut. A veteran of the French and Indian War, he placed himself at the head of a company of Connecticut volunteers when the Revolution began and set out to Boston to offer himself to the cause.

Arnold went to the American headquarters at Cambridge and met with the Massachusetts Committee of Safety, which was acting as the provisional government of the colony, and laid his plan before them; he would capture Fort Ticonderoga for the Americans.

The committee authorized this step and gave him a commission as colonel. Arnold already had a fine uniform. Despite his business ventures he had a yen for the military, and his dashing uniform and his valet doubtless impressed the committee. He was 33 years old, with a compulsion to command, and the committee gave him a hundred pounds in cash, a little ammunition, and the authority to raise 400 men. On May 3 he set out for Lake Champlain agog with excitement at the thought of capturing Fort Ticonderoga and becoming a hero. At the same moment Ethan Allen, over in Bennington, was laying his plans to do the same thing.

On Monday, May 8, the aspiring heroes collided. Ethan had left Bennington and set out for Shoreham, where he found things progressing well. It had been decided that at daybreak on May 10 the attack would be made, launched from Hands Cove at Shoreham. Troops were moving toward the spot, and other Green Mountain Boys were seizing all the boats they could to move the men across the water of the lake to the fort. All was ready when into Castleton rode Benedict Arnold, spurred and uniformed, commission in hand, and escorted only by his body servant. As he had ridden toward Bennington reports reached him that somebody else was mustering troops, so Arnold nobly rushed forward to assume command, not bothering to raise any more men.

The committee of war was just about to adjourn when Arnold rode in and presented his credentials for taking charge. The committee was at first astonished and then furious. Their leader, Ethan Allen, was already heading for the front, they shouted.

Arnold then set out for Shoreham where he found Allen and his Green Mountain Boys in their shabby woodsmen's garb. Allen was taken aback. After all, this interloper did have credentials, and Allen had none. He almost gave in, but when his men staunchly refused to serve under Arnold, Ethan regained his confidence. He even felt a little sorry for Arnold, and doing the diplomatic thing he made a bizarre decision. Arnold would be allowed in the act too; he could march side by side with Allen at the head of the force but not in a command position of the 230 men who would take orders only from their chosen commander.

So at eleven o'clock the night of May 9, 1775, Allen, his loyal troops, and the overdressed and fuming Col. Arnold with his certificate in hand waited for the commandeered boats to take them across for the proposed early morning capture of the fort in the first offensive action of the American Revolution.

Actually, other documents have indicated that Allen first collared a Lt. Jocelyn Feltham, mistaking him for the captain, and that Delaplace, fully and elaborately uniformed, appeared moments later to officially give up the fort to the Americans and to present his sword to Col. Ethan Allen of the Green Mountain Boys. Ticonderoga had been won with no loss of life by a hardy bunch of future Vermonters who had accomplished the impossible, capturing a strategic fort that had cost the British government eight million sterling.

By mid-morning the rest of the troops arrived. They were in haste to get to the fort because word was out that a great amount of rum was stored there and Allen, to Arnold's indignation, thought the troops should have a little merriment and reward for their work.

But there was more work still to be done, as Crown Point had to be taken. Responsible Seth Warner, who had missed the capture (as he commanded the last of the crossings) was dispatched with a party to Crown Point. There he ran into Remember Baker hurrying in from the north. Baker helped secure Crown Point, disappointed that word had not reached him in time for the big show at Fort Ticonderoga.

At about the same time, a number of boats were captured at Skenesboro, including a schooner owned by Col. Philip Skene. The loot was important. Altogether the Green Mountain Boys got 200 cannons, howitzers, mortars, ammunition, food supplies and the celebrated rum. They also took over 60 prisoners — and about 40 women and children who were gallantly treated by Ethan.

38. Fort Ticonderoga Is Seized — 1775

Ethan Allen had never been inside Fort Ticonderoga, so he needed a guide. According to historian Henry DuPuy, Nathan Beeman, a youth who lived on a farm near the fort, had spent many hours with the "boys of the garrison." As he knew every passage and approach to the fort, he agreed, upon the persuasion of his father and Colonel Allen, to lead them in.

The few boats that had been commandeered from Skenesboro had only carried over 83 men when light began to show along the horizon. Allen decided not to wait for the rest of the troops but to attack at once. According to his own later account Allen "harangued" his men in a flowery speech, a doubtful but if true, risky procedure, for he could have been heard by the sentries. But Ethan liked to write out speeches in retrospect, so he records his remarks in part:" ... I now propose to advance before you, and, in person, conduct you through the wicket-gate; for we must this morning either quit our pretensions to valor, or possess ourselves of this fortress in a few minutes ... "

The inspired men followed their leader and his unwelcome assistant Col. Arnold; the company crept up the height to the sally port when the sentinel snapped his fusee, which was aimed at Allen, but it failed to fire. The fellow retreated into the fort under the covered way, Americans following. There another sentinel made a thrust, but Allen downed him with a blow of his sword. The Green Mountain Boys rushed yelling into the parade. As sleeping British soldiers were aroused and captured by the invaders, Allen shouted for the commandant to surrender.

Allen writes that he pushed up the stairs and immediately saw Capt. William Delaplace at the top of the steps with his breeches in his hand. Delaplace demanded to know to what authority he was to surrender. Allen says he uttered those ringing words dear to all Vermonters, "In the name of the

Great Jehovah and the Continental Congress."

Some say he didn't say any such thing but instead ripped off some unprintable epithets. But Allen, writing in his *Narrative*, reports he said just that. Some people have said that Delaplace had about as much respect for the Continental Congress as Allen had for Jehovah. Whatever the words, it was a dramatic moment.

39. Arnold and Allen — 1775

On the morning of May 10, 1775, Forth Ticonderoga was filled with milling men (some with hangovers, no doubt), prisoners, and two leaders who were obviously not getting along. Allen had allowed Arnold to walk in beside him, but he did not by any means consider him a co-commander.

Arnold did not like the way things were going. He felt that the Green Mountain Boys were most unmilitary, and Arnold was strong on military etiquette. The Green Mountain Boys thought this was funny. The poked Arnold with their guns and made rude remarks to him which punctured his dignity, so Colonel Arnold retired to a corner and fumed and sulked. After all, the men there were Ethan's soldiers, and Benedict had nobody to command.

Ethan was in his glory. The men loved him. The success was unqualified, and he sat down to write letters to the Continental Congress and to the provincial congresses in Connecticut, Massachusetts, and New York as well as to his friends back home. Ethan was honestly worried that when Canada heard the news, it might send a great force down to retake the prize, and he wanted support.

He was particularly concerned about a British sloop which was cruising Lake Champlain from its station at the British stronghold of St. Johns up on the Sorel (Richelieu) River. It would be a good move to capture it and the troops at St. Johns, and on this Arnold and Allen agreed. When boats arrived from Skenesboro a few days later, and a hundred men appeared to serve under Arnold, he was dispatched down the lake (which means heading north in this case) to take over St. Johns.

Arnold, who had had experience with ships, did well. He captured the British sloop which was at anchor at St. Johns and then went in to take 13 prisoners. On the way back, captured vessel in tow, they met Ethan Allen and about a hundred Green Mountain Boys crowded into four batteaux, rowing their way downstream.

Evidently Allen intended to share the victory with Arnold, but he was too late. Allen glosses over these details in his *Narrative*, but he writes that he went aboard Arnold's ship and the two drank the health of the new country. Allen told Arnold of his plan to keep on down the lake and to take possession of St. Johns to use as a base of operations against Canada. Arnold writes that he advised against this, but Allen persisted.

That night, the Green Mountain Boys and their leader, hungry and exhausted, slept on the ground opposite St. Johns, resting for the next move. They were aroused at daybreak by gunfire from British troops from Montreal who had arrived to aid the fort. The confused Green Mountain Boys piled into boats and beat their way south. In the haste of departure three men were left behind. It was humiliating, and it was the beginning of Ethan's loss of the confidence in which he had been held by the people of the Grants.

It was now nearly June, and the farmers had to be at home planting. Allen's troops began deserting in droves. Allen had nothing to do but to turn things over to Arnold, who now had some reliable hired men under his control. On May 27 Allen stepped down. More troubles were brewing. The Continental Congress, which had not authorized the attack on Fort Ticonderoga to begin with, began to consider the brashness of it all. They decided that the captured guns should be returned to the British. This raised such a public outcry that the order was rescinded, but they were still fearful and not supportive of these tempestuous Green Mountain Boys.

If the fort were abandoned, the people in the Grants would be totally unprotected against the now righteously indignant and strategically placed British troops from Canada. Ethan, completely committed to the invasion of Canada, as he felt that it could be taken with little difficulty, hoped to stir up sympathy for the Americans among the French Canadians. They lost no love for the British government which had controlled them since the peace of 1763 when France pulled out of Canada, and Allen placed undue confidence in this.

40. The Canadian Campaign — 1775

The French Canadians, whom Ethan wished to court as allies for the rebellious colonies, had been mortal enemies of the New England settlers in the French and Indian wars. There was not much time to patch up a century of hostility there, but Ethan had heard that the French Canadians were deeply aggrieved at the British rule. Gov. Sir Guy Carlton, recorded in history as a man of highest intelligence and integrity, had masterminded the Quebec Act, designed to give justice to both the French habitants and the American colonists, but it pleased nobody. The colonists felt it undid the treaty of 1763, and the French Canadians felt they were being Anglicized. Ethan chuckled to hear that the French Canadians in a fit of rage demonstrated against the British government on May 1, 1775, by solemnly marching through Montreal to urinate one by one on the statue of George III.

So Ethan, with the conquest of Canada in mind, sent some emissaries up to try to establish quick friendships, but the cautious Canadians never caught the secession fever from the other colonies, despite some protest over the Stamp Act in 1765. Ethan believed that the Canadians would support him; this was the second great blunder of judgment, the first being his abortive attempt to seize St. Johns.

The French habitants were indifferent to the overtures.

They listened to their priests who supported the British rule which in turn supported them. The fur traders liked nothing better than to see the British colonies south of Canada at war with the mother country. This would give them the entire fur market. And so the stage was set for a sad drama for Ethan Allen.

In June relations between Arnold and Allen at Fort Ticonderoga were so strained that Allen decided to go to the Continental Congress and lay matters before them; so with Seth Warner he arrived in Philadelphia on June 22 to tell them about it. Ethan must have done well, for the Congress of the United Colonies of America recommended to the Convention of New York that they employ the Green Mountain Boys for the defense of America, under the general command of General Philip Schuyler, but with other officers of their own choosing. New York was to pay the troops for the Ticonderoga expedition and a hesitant agreement was made for the invasion of Canada.

Less than a year before, prices had been put on the heads of the leaders of the Green Mountain Boys by this very Convention of New York. Ethan and Seth could scarcely contain their astonishment at their success with the men in Philadelphia. Brazening it out, they took their papers from the Philadelphia congress and proceeded to New York City where the convention sat, not knowing whether they would be arrested. It was just the sort of brinksmanship that Ethan relished. However, New York realized that the brash Green Mountain Boys could be stalwart protectors in case the British moved up the lake, and the seizure of Fort Ticonderoga had been to the advantage of New York.

When Allen and Warner got to New York they had to wait outside for an hour while the assembly decided whether or not to admit them. Once admitted, Allen made a convincing case and came out the winner: he was to raise, at New York's expense, a regiment of not more than seven companies totalling 500 men. They would receive back pay, and later it was voted to purchase green cloth to provide a coat for each member and to furnish red facings for the coats, and to supply tents, and ammunition. Money was advanced for blankets. At last the Green Mountain Boys had become respectable.

41. Ethan's Defeat — 1775

On July 26, 1775, the committees of "several townships" met at Cephas Kent's house in Dorset to choose the field officers for the Green Mountain Boys. On May 23 the New York provincial congress had met, called by a committee of 100, to withstand the strong Tory party in New York. Obviously they realized that New York would be as vulnerable to attack from Canada as the Grants, and that the Green Mountain Boys were their best protection. Tories were always strong in New York State, and fighting with them continued long after the Revolution was virtually over. Considering the aristocratic attitude of Yorkers during the squabble with the Grants, it is rather surprising that they did become a party to the patriot cause.

Nathan Clark was chosen chairman of the Dorset convention. Ethan Allen of course was expecting to be chosen colonel of the regiment. Even today one shares the chagrin that overwhelmed Ethan Allen, hero of Fort Ticonderoga, protector of liberty, as he heard Seth Warner elected to the post that he felt was his by right. Then he listened dizzily as he heard seven captains, seven lieutenants and seven second lieutenants chosen, and not even a lowly niche for himself. Warner was chosen by a majority of 41-5.

Ethan, now 40 years old, blamed this stunning defeat on "the old farmers," but it probably had to do with errors in judgment and a general brashness that could be disastrous in the awesome conflict in prospect. His brothers Heman, Ira, and Ebeneazer were all given offices.

Allen took the blow in good fashion. He did not lose his enthusiasm for the cause. Not one to sit and sulk, he acted; a few days after the embarrassing vote he visited General

Schuyler and offered his services. The Green Mountain Boys supported their former leader and persuaded the general to allow Ethan to go along as scout on the proposed Canadian expedition.

It was late August before Schuyler decided to act. Finally it turned out that his gout was bad and he was too old to lead the rough expedition, so the command went to General Archibald Montgomery, famous for being with Wolfe at the taking of Quebec in 1759. He had resigned his commission in the British Amry and emigrated to America.

Ethan, who was sent ahead to persuade the Canadians to rise up and help the Americans, did well with this assignment and actually did raise an army of Canadians, most of whom he sent to join Montgomery at St. Johns. As preparations for the invasion progressed, Ethan had an additional personal sorrow when he learned that Remember Baker, his cousin and close friend, had been killed by the Indians. On a scouting expedition near St. Johns in August, Baker was ambushed, shot, and beheaded. The Caughnawgas were carrying his head around on a pole, proud of their trophy, until the British persuaded them to give it up for burial. Remember had not been chosen for an office in the Green Mountain Boys, either, and the death of his fellow scout was a sad blow to Ethan.

On September 18 Ethan was recruiting right under the nose of authority, and Gov. Guy Carlton was well aware of it. Major John Brown, also out scouting, met Allen, and they cooked up a plan, according to Allen's *Narrative*, that they go ahead and capture Montreal themselves, not waiting for orders and more troops. Brown and Allen and their limited troops were to converge on the city on a prearranged signal.

According to Allen, Brown failed to carry out his side of the bargain. Allen with 110 men, only part of whom had gotten across the river, had to go it alone. On the morning of September 25, 1775, daylight caught Allen unable to retreat, a miserable fiasco. Allen surrendered and was brought to General Richard Prescott, that apoplectic American-hater who was noted for shaking his fist and shouting "disperse, ye rebels," at the sight of Americans. Prescott ordered the

Canadians shot, but Allen interceded for them. An Indian tried to kill Allen, but that was avoided too. Allen was put in chains on the British ship *Gaspee*, and sent to prison in England.

Brown's previous and subsequent records are not consistent with Allen's accusations. It has never been satisfactorily explained what happened that night when Brown failed Allen at Montreal. When Ethan returned from prison three years later, everyone was much too busy with other matters to find out the facts for history.

42. Military Matters — July 1776

Things were happening in all corners of the land between the Connecticut River and Lake Champlain when the Continental Congress in Philadelphia signed the Declaration of Independence on July 4, 1776. For one thing, men of Vermont were meeting that month in Dorset, for the third time.

The Green Mountain Boys had pulled out of Canada and holed up at Fort Ticonderoga and at the new and unnamed fort across the narrow waters of Lake Champlain on the eastern shore. On July 12, General Horatio Gates, now in charge of the Northern Army, decided to abandon Crown Point, to the distress of the settlers in the area. Indian attacks were more to be feared than British attacks, and most people were scared stiff.

On July 28, soldiers, working hard to make the new fort as attack-proof as possible, were called together in general quarters after a messenger clattered up to the gate. Laying down their shovels and trowels they surged into the parade to hear the proclamation of their commanding officer, Col. Arthur St. Clair. Down in Philadelphia on July 4, they heard, a Declaration of Independence had been signed by the members of the Continental Congress. The representatives there had declared the ties with England broken and had pledged themselves to fight for independence. Of course, the Grants had no representatives there, but the soldiers were fighting for those very principles, and had been since the Green Mountain Boys had seized Fort Ticonderoga. They broke into loud huzzahs, danced about with high spirits, and shouted even louder when their commandant declared that the new fort would from this moment on be known as Fort Independence.

"Now we are a people; we have a name among the States of the world," said one old letter from that day and place. (A note on the speed of news in those days: although it was July 28 when the word reached the new fort, it was first read on August 5 in Richmond and August 11 in Boston.)

Although Lake Champlain seemed the most vulnerable part of the Grants to British attack, there was action in the eastern part as well. Jacob Bayley, the most prominent man in the eastern area, proposed to Gen. George Washington that a military road be built to Canada beginning at Wells River. Washington agreed with this plan, but Bayley had to pay for it himself. Of such stuff were patriots in those days. The road never got beyond Hazen's Notch, but the military activity no doubt deterred an invasion into that area. Bayley became a general in the Continental Army as a commissary and logistics specialist. A monument to him is on the common at Newbury.

A methodical man, intelligent and experienced in warfare and government, he consistently opposed Ethan Allen. He was as cautious as Allen was brash, but finally their differences were resolved when they both became official "Vermonters." The history of Vermont was not entirely the history of the Allen family.

General Schuyler, who had preceded General Gates as head of the Northern Army, was from a prominent New York family and never got over his mistrust of the Green Mountain Boys, although they served under him bravely in the 1775 campaign. However, Schuyler, an experienced soldier from the French and Indian Wars, proclaimed that the actions of George III were grievous, and he thundered out for joining the other colonies. His patriotic American attitude helped lead to New York's first anti-Tory congress on May 23, 1775.

43. The Battle of Valcour — 1776

In the summer of 1776 boats were being built and readied on Lake Champlain by workers at Fort Ticonderoga. Further down the lake the British were building boats, too, for there was going to be a confrontation, no doubt about it. But there was a little personal squabble to settle first.

General Gates, often a contentious figure, selected Arnold to take charge of the American fleet, and at the same time General Schuyler picked one Jacobus Wynkoop for the same job. Schuyler and Wynkoop were both Dutch, methodical, and dependable. Wynkoop got there first, but evidently he did little for the fleet except shine the motley array of vessels. General Gates replaced Wynkoop with Benedict Arnold, a delicate matter since Schuyler was still nominally in command.

When Arnold, acting on Gates' orders, tried to relieve Wynkoop with no success, General Gates ordered Wynkoop arrested and taken to Albany. (Later he returned to be captain of a schooner under Arnold.) Vain, cantankerous, and disliked as he was, Arnold was still brilliant and efficient, and the Americans needed him.

Arnold sent to the New England seaports for experienced ships' carpenters and a supply of naval stores, and he pushed like a madman, inspiring his men to work day and night to get some kind of fleet ready to sail.

At the prow of his flagship, *The Royal Savage*, on August 24, 1776, Arnold led his fleet of three schooners, two sloops, three galleys, and eight gondolas out of unfortified Crown Point. A dreadful nor'easter arose, but the fleet rode it out, and by September 2 they were gathered at Windmill Point with the British only four or five miles north.

89

Arnold decided to make a stand on October 11 at Valcour Island, which lies in Lake Champlain west of South Hero and is now part of New York State. He managed to conceal his ships at the upper end of the island while the British sailed south with more than 70 vessels with 93 guns and 700 seamen. Greatly outnumbered in ships, guns, and men, Arnold fought bravely; military experts consider his tactics brilliant. The British thought they had hemmed him in after the first day of fighting, but the American fleet slipped though the British line that night.

Arnold would not accept the word defeat. The British fleet was badly damaged, and the American fleet went down fighting when Arnold destroyed most of his ships rather than let them be taken. He had fought against outrageous odds. Refusing to fall into the hands of the enemy, he finally ran his remaining ships ashore, ordering his men to leap overboard as he set the last ships on fire. Dramatically he emerged as the last man from the smoke-enveloped flagship. He took his survivors back to Fort Ticonderoga on foot. Only one ship had been captured.

Arnold was an instant hero, but due to his bad relations with fellow generals, especially Horatio Gates, he was passed over for the promotion he expected. This caused a bitterness bordering on madness, and he eventually betrayed his country by selling out West Point to the British. He escaped to join the British Army and fight against his old country, even burning New London, his former home. He died a broken but wealthy man in 1801.

The defeat was a victory in that Lake Champlain was not taken by the British in 1776, giving the Americans a little more time for greater conflicts to come.

General Carlton managed to sail up to Crown Point, but after two weeks in the area he turned back without attacking since he feared being trapped by ice before reinforcements could come. His ships and men were too much damaged by Arnold's spunky little navy to attack without more help.

44. Government by Conventions — 1766-1775

If the New Hampshire Grants had not had a dedicated group of intelligent citizens during the long struggle for control of the area, it could never have become a state. For about a decade the Grants were governed by conventions of citizens, a remarkable record of men working for the common good. Because this was happening when the larger and better publicized story of the beginnings of the United States overwhelmed the press, not many people have much knowledge of Vermont's government by conventions.

Doubtless there were many public indignation meetings that were not recorded, for at first some meetings were spontaneous and informal, becoming more organized and legalistic as independence developed. Considering the roads, it is remarkable that delegates got to the meetings which were often in winter, always a sacrifice in time and money for farmers who paid their own expenses. They had few books and little education, but delegates read their John Locke books to shreds and listened excitedly to the ideas of Thomas Paine and Benjamin Franklin which seeped in by occasional travellers or out-of-date newspapers.

In 1776 after New York began usurping Grants land right and left in defiance of a royal order of 1764, the settlers of Pownal, Bennington, Shaftsbury, Arlington, Sunderland, Manchester, and Danby decided to pool their resistance and appoint an agent to take their case to the king. They met in Bennington, and a petition with over 1,000 signatures was prepared for Samuel Robinson, a prominent man of the town, to take to England. Mr. Robinson, a man of 60, died in England, but not before he accomplished his mission. The king reversed his decision and sent word to New York to stop all activity in the Grants.

The people were elated; cooperation of towns had won the day. When New York chose to defy the king's decision, Grants people had a meeting of public concern in May 1770 to decide what to do. Ethan Allen had now arrived in the Grants, and a group of citizens met at Fay's Tavern in Bennington and chose him to act as an agent for the area to see if New Hampshire would help.

When Ethan returned from New Hampshire in October 1770, the people met again and decided to raise a military company and use force to protect their property. As we have seen, this was the birth of the Green Mountain Boys with Ethan Allen in command. Ira Allen, Ethan's youngest brother, wrote: "This was a bold stroke of a hundred men, who united to oppose the most favored colony under the Crown, and whose wealth and numbers were great."

There is a record of a meeting in Manchester in 1774, which adjourned to meet in Arlington, listing resolutions against the conduct of New York. Then the people of Westminster had met on April 11, 1775, to protest New York's actions. But the first well-documented official convention was held at Dorset on July 26, 1775.

On December 10, 1775, another convention of citizens of the Grants was formally warned when a warrant was sent out by a committee of seven men to notify the people west of the Green Mountains that there would be a convention on January 16, 1776, in Dorset to decide whether the law of New York should have free circulation where it would not interfere with the New Hampshire titles or the defense of the titles. Further, the convention was to decide if they, the convened body, could take action on "schismatic Mobbs" that might arise. That last phrase in itself indicates the borderline of anarchy in the area and the necessity of men taking over their own government. Further, they wished to act on sending an agent to the Continental Congress in Philadelphia, and to see if the Grants would "associate" with New York or act as their own body in "the cause of America." They were assuming an unusual degree of power.

After choosing officers and committees, they decided that only two persons from each town could vote in that meeting, but in the future votes would be representative of the populations of the 18 towns involved.

It was voted to lay the case of the Grants before the Continental Congress, and Heman Allen was elected to take the matter to them with a "remonstrance" composed by a committee of seven. The power to call further meetings was given to two regional committees, and the convention voted that they would do all in their power for the general cause of the colonies under the Continental Congress, but they would not put themselves under the supervision of New York.

The following May when the roads were passable Heman Allen took the "remonstrance" to Philadelphia to the Continental Congress. It was turned over to a committee, but when it appeared that the committee would act unfavorably on it Heman very wisely withdrew it and returned to Vermont.

45. The Convention and Association of July 1776

The Declaration of Independence was signed in July 1776 in Philadelphia just before the next convention in the Grants on July 24, 1776, but it is doubtful if word of Congress's action had been received in Dorset when the delegates assembled. This time 31 towns with 51 delegates gathered, including a town from the east. Townshend was represented by Capt. Samuel Fletcher and Josiah Fish, the first time any "easterners" had attended a convention.

The first items of business give a clue to the mood of conventions of the day. "Voted: First. That not more than one person be allowed to speak at the same time, and only by leave of the chairman. Second. That the business of the meeting be closely attended to."

Then Heman Allen read the remonstrance he had taken down to Congress, since the delegates had not heard it before. Further, he told of the movement for independence throughout the colonies and the good news that a few people in

Philadelphia supported the independence movement in the Grants as well.

So far nothing had been said about a treasury, but some funds must have been contributed, for a motion was made to pay Heman Allen. Another motion was made to poll the people of the Grants to get their reaction to forming a separate district. This was the first official and recorded act toward independence for the Grants.

In July 1776 groups were forming "associations" to declare their intentions toward Great Britain. The Declaration of Independence in Philadelphia was such an association, and New York now had a pact, too. But the Grants people, while being completely in accord with independence from England, were not willing to sign a compact of independence in conjunction with New York. Accordingly, 49 members of the July 24, 1776, convention at Dorset signed an association as follows:

"We, the subscribers, inhabitants of the district of land, commonly called and known by the name of the New Hampshire Grants, do voluntarily and solemnly engage under all the ties held sacred amongst mankind, at the risque of our lives and fortunes, to defend by arms the United American States against the hostile attempts of the British fleets and armies, until the present unhappy controversy between the two countries shall be settled."

The convention further recommended that the people who subscribed to another covenant (especially New York's) "be deemed enemies to the common cause of the New Hampshire Grants." The convention then set up a committee to act as a court of appeals for determining judgments brought up from town committees, a giant step toward independence. The convention then adjourned until September with instructions for the delegates to get their constituents to sign the general association and bring it back to the clerk.

While the July 1776 Convention was sitting at Dorset, the Americans had retreated from Canada and had holed up, sick and discouraged, at Fort Ticonderoga and at the new Fort Independence. Crown Point was evacuated. Benedict Arnold was preparing to fight a naval battle on Lake Champlain, and things looked bad for the Grants. The desperation of the undefended frontier, the cupidity of New York, the indecision of the Continental Congress, and the indifference of New Hampshire perhaps served in this hour of peril to bring out the best in the men who acted so decisively at that historic convention.

46. More Conventions for Statehood — 1776

When September 25, 1776, came and the 56 delegates from 33 towns began to arrive at Cephas Kent's in Dorset, there was a change in the crowd. Ten towns were represented from the east, and this time the theme was openly for statehood for the Grants, east and west.

When it came time to vote on the measure brought up at the last meeting, that "suitable application be made to form that district of land commonly called and known by the name of New Hampshire Grants, into a separate district," it passed without a dissenting vote.

Since the military situation was desperate at this moment, the delegates made a covenant giving the convention the power to rule — at least temporarily. This was an act enabling the convention to govern the Grants, subject to "the principles of Congress." New York's jurisdiction was completely repudiated, and in effect the New Hampshire Grants became a new political entity. Every male over 16 was to sign or make his mark on the "association" so that the collected signatures could be returned to the clerk. In all, 47 items were voted upon including the decision to build a jail, appoint a jail keeper and to make a census of the men in military service. Further, the report of this convention and a "Remonstrance" or Petition was to be sent to the Continental Congress.

What made this probably the most important of all the early conventions was the decision that the matter of statehood was to be taken home to the people for their opinion.

This was not a matter of formal voting at polls, but nevertheless, it was a democratic gesture in keeping with the sentiments of the Grants' people.

The chairman of the September convention was Joseph Bowker, who had been chosen in the July 24, 1776 convention and had continued in the office through December 24, 1777, as far as the records note. Bowker, from Rutland, had settled under a New Hampshire Grant and opposed New York from the start. A trusted man, he later became a member of the governor's council and held judgeships and other important state offices before his death in 1784.

The convention adjourned to meet again at Westminster on October 30, 1776. The move to Westminster, after four conventions at Dorset, was a political one to entice the eastern Vermonters to take even more of a part in the proceedings.

It was clear that the October meeting was intended for voting the new state into being when the delegates returned with the word of the people, but most of the able-bodied men of the Grants were fighting for their lives and property in October 1776. Over 13,000 men were assembled at Fort Ticonderoga and Fort Independence to thwart the drive of Gen. Guy Carleton who was moving south on Lake Champlain. Benedict Arnold had just fought the Battle of Valcour and had scuttled the fleet. Col. Seth Warner and Gen. Horatio Gates expected the worst, a full scale invasion from Canada, so the vote for statehood was postponed for more immediate matters until January.

47. New Connecticut and a Declaration of Independence — 1777

Impressed by the mass of men gathered at Fort Ticonderoga and Fort Independence in the autumn of 1776, General Carlton, fearful of being trapped in a frozen lake before reinforcements could reach him, turned back to Montreal.

This gave the men of the Grants time to turn their thoughts to the most celebrated of all their conventions, which began January 15, 1777, in Westminster. Nineteen towns were represented by 22 people, and some towns sent in letters to vote for the new state, for that was the avowed purpose of the session.

Routine business being disposed of on the first day, on January 16 the meeting was called to order at eight in the morning. It was probably dark, with candles lighting the court house. Ebeneazer Hosington, chairman of the committee to examine votes, reported: "We find by examination that more than three-fourths of the people in Cumberland and Gloucester Counties, that have acted, are for a new state; the rest we view as neuters."

And then the meeting was adjourned for an hour.

After a lunch break the gentlemen reconvened and voted for statehood.

The minutes of the meeting say: "*6th. Voted, N.C.D., That the district of land commonly called and known by the name of New Hampshire Grants, be a new and separate state; and for the future conduct themselves as such.*"

Then committees were chosen to draw a plan for "further proceedings" and to draft a declaration of independence. The draft for the declaration was brought to the floor early the next day.

The committee listed the rights of the convention to declare statehood. The paper set forth the contention that when protection was withheld, no allegiance was due; that New York had treated the Grants' people badly; that its citizens were now free people; that a government would be formed to protect the rights of the people and would be established at the next convention. They named the state New Connecticut.

A point in the report was that the right to form the state of New Connecticut came from the Continental Congress itself. On May 15, 1776, John Adams had put through a resolution that "where no government sufficient to the exigences of their affairs hath been hitherto established, to adopt such government, as shall, in the opinion of the representatives of the people best conduce to the happiness and safety of their constituents in particular and to America in general."

On Friday morning, January 17, 1777, the committee brought in a long report listing the rights of the people of the Grants and concluding with Vermont's Declaration of Independence as follows:

"This Convention whose members are duly chosen by the free voice of their constituents in the several towns, on the New Hampshire Grants, in public meeting assembled, in our own names, and in behalf of our constituents, do hereby proclaim and publicly declare that the district of territory comprehending and usually known by the name and description of the New Hampshire Grants, of right ought to be, and is hereby declared forever hereafter to be considered as a separate, free and independent jurisdiction or state; by the name, and forever hereafter to be called, known and distinguished by the name of NEW CONNECTICUT; and that the inhabitants that at present are, or that hereafter may become resident, either by procreation or emigration, within said territory, shall be entitled to the same privileges, immunities, and enfranchisements as are allowed; and on such condition, and in the same manner, as the present inhabitants in future shall or may enjoy; which are, and forever shall be considered, to be such privileges and immunities to the free citizens and denizens as are, or, at any time hereafter, may be allowed to any such inhabitants of any of the free and independent states of America; And that such privileges and immunities shall be regulated by a bill of rights, and by a form of government, to be established at the next adjourned session of this convention."

Voted: To accept the above declaration.

48. Vermont is Named — 1777

Dr. Jones Fay, Col. Thomas Chittenden, Dr. Reuben Jones, Col. Jacob Bayley, and Capt. Heman Allen were chosen at the January 1777 convention to take up the matter of new statehood with the Continental Congress. Heman Allen had been there before with no luck, but this time the situation was more hopeful. This group of the Grants' most distinguished men wanted recognition of the independence of New Connecticut as well as representation in the Congress. But due to New York's influence Congress was already disposed to turn down New Connecticut's petition.

Despite their disappointment a significant bit of luck came from encountering an old friend of the Allen's, Dr. Thomas Young. Dr. Young had lived in Dutchess County, New York, when Ethan Allen was living in Salisbury, Connecticut, and the two men had become boon companions, spending hours arguing the validity of the Bible and talking down organized religion. They began to write the book which in later years Ethan published as *The Oracles of Reason.*

Dr. Young, who had moved from New York to Boston and finally to Philadelphia, was an ardent patriot and was delighted to see his old friends from the Grants. He took up their cause at once. While New York and her powerful friends worked against the new state, Dr. Young came through with high encouragement, promises, and ideas. He even produced a constitution, ready-made for the new state. But there was already a New Connecticut in Pennsylvania he told them. Why not name the new state VERMONT?

The visitors were elated. Vermont! What a fine name — new, like the state — and it had a real meaning for it was taken from the French words *Verd Mont*, meaning Green Mountain.

The constitution of Vermont, said Dr. Young, could be patterned after the new constitution of Pennsylvania. That document, he continued excitedly, was a model of liberal government, framed just the year before by Benjamin Franklin

99

and Thomas Paine and other forward thinking men. It would fit the needs of Vermont perfectly.

Furthermore, Dr. Young penned a letter (a copy of which still exists) stating that he would use his utmost influence in the Congress, and that if Vermont would properly elect delegates to a constitutional convention in the state and would adopt a constitution such as the one he was furnishing, he was quite sure that they would be admitted to the congress of states.

"I tell you to organize fairly, and make the experiment, and I will ensure your success at the risk of my reputation as a man of honor or commonsense. Indeed they can by no means refuse you!"

The Vermonters hurried back to Windsor where the June 4, 1777, convention was to meet, with the letter from Dr. Young and a copy of the Pennsylvania Constitution. The new name Vermont was unanimously adopted by the 72 delegates present who eagerly read and discussed the proposed constitution. Towns were instructed to choose their delegates on June 23 for a convention to be held in Windsor in early July 1777.

However, military matters were on everyone's mind. Gen. John Burgoyne was moving toward Fort Ticonderoga, and the settlers were in a panic. A proclamation was read to observe June 18 as a day of prayer and fasting. Evil times seemed to lie ahead for the new state of Vermont.

49. Vermont Gets a Constitution — 1777

Not many people turned up for the July 2, 1777, convention at Windsor, although delegates had been duly chosen to meet and adopt a constitution for the new state of Vermont.

War clouds were frighteningly close. Burgoyne was at Crown Point, and intelligence gatherers found out that he was planning to push south down the Hudson to join forces with General Howe who would move north from New York.

Lord George Germain, the colonial secretary in London, wrote to General Burgoyne: "With a view of quelling the rebellion as soon as possible, it is highly necessary that the most speedy junction of the two armies should be effected." The plan was to cut the colonies in half and thus put down "the rebellion."

The Green Mountain Boys had a surprise in store for Burgoyne, who was later to write: "The New Hampshire Grants, in particular, a country unpeopled in the last war [meaning the French and Indian Wars], now abounds in the most active and most rebellious race on the continent, and hangs like a gathering storm on my left."

At Windsor there was nervous excitement among the 34 delegates from 28 towns. On sultry, hot July 8 a draft of the Constitution lay before the exhausted men. A rider dashed into the courtyard and leaped from his horse just ahead of a violent thunderclap.

"Our forces have evacuated Fort Ti!" he shouted. "There's fighting at Hubbardton. Every man's needed!"

There was pandemonium in the meeting as the delegates tipped over their chairs, shouted, and looked at each other in alarm. Although complete minutes of this dramatic convention have never been found, letters and other documents helped reconstruct the scene. Chairman Joseph Bowker, a man of sound judgment, realized the importance of getting the Constitution approved while the delegates were assembled. If they all dispersed to grab a gun, then the very thing they were fighting for would be lost at the outset.

"Gentlemen," he probably said, "torrents of rain are beginning to fall. Let us wind this thing up first, and then disband."

And they did. They resolved the last of the differences on the document, approved it unanimously, and remembered that they must have a Council of Safety to rule Vermont until an election could be held under the government they had just authorized. Elections were scheduled for December 1777.

The rain stopped, the new Constitution of the State of Vermont was turned over to Ira Allen so that he could get it printed for the people to see, and then men set out for home as fast as possible. Thomas Chittenden, who would soon be elected president of the Council of Safety, had especial cause for alarm, for his unprotected family was in the line of march of the British forces, as were the families of at least a dozen of the other representatives.

50. The Battle of Hubbardton — 1777

Burgoyne was especially frightening to the Vermonters since he had stirred up the Indians. "Gentleman Johnny" Burgoyne as he was called, according to Lossing's *Field Book of the Revolution*, was the illegitimate son of Lord Bingley. Bright, brash, luxury loving, and eventually a successful dramatist in London, he was put in the army very young and his good family connections put him in line for easy promotions.

There were grumbles when he replaced Sir Guy Carlton in Canada in 1777. Vermonters generally trusted Carlton even though he was an enemy. Burgoyne sent out a pompous proclamation to the inhabitants of the Hubbardton, Rutland, Tinmouth, Pawlet district ordering the inhabitants to turn themselves in or be executed.

"I have but to give stretch to the Indian forces under my direction, and they amount to thousands," announced Burgoyne, "to overtake the enemies of Great Britain and America."

The patriots may have secretly quaked in their boots, but outwardly they were contemptuous. Military action on Lake Champlain developed quickly in 1777. In June Burgoyne had assembled an army of 7,000 in Canada, half of which were German. True to his threat, Burgoyne also raised 500 Iroquois Indians and held a council of war, hoping to incite them to kill the Americans. He promised a bounty for scalps taken from the dead, but he made the fine distinction of asking them not to take scalps from the living. Even this gesture did not cheer up the Vermonters.

Then Burgoyne began to move up the lake. General Schuyler, the only Yorker the Vermonters could tolerate, was put in charge of the Northern Army of the continental forces. Schuyler found things in bad shape when he arrived at Fort Ticonderoga in June, so leaving Gen. Arthur St. Clair in charge, he went to Fort Edward for supplies and men.

General St. Clair was a Scotsman, "an excellent and able man, full of integrity, just and kind. He possessed talents, but no genius, and was never made for a military character of our times," says T.J. Headley who wrote about the Revolutionary War generals. St. Clair had served with Wolfe in Canada and stayed on to become part of the American Army.

St. Clair's lack of genius was immediately manifested in his failure to fortify a high hill that overlooked Fort Ticonderoga and Fort Independence. Called Sugar Hill or Mount Defiance, it rose so steeply that St. Clair assumed that the British could never fortify it, but on the morning of July 5 the Americans found the British all dug in overlooking the American forts.

The year before Burgoyne arrived, the Americans had built Fort Independence across the lake on the Vermont side and had now completed a floating bridge over the narrow strip of water that divided the two forts. There was no choice but to evacuate both installations, since the Americans were understaffed, undersupplied, and surprised. Actually, some leaders had thought Burgoyne was only scaring them and that the major thrust would come on the eastern seaboard.

St. Clair arranged a rather remarkable retreat. In the early morning on July 6 the troops from Fort Ticonderoga crept over the floating bridge and joined with the troops at Fort Independence, and all of them cautiously crept down the heights and beat a retreat toward Castleton. They were so skillful that their evacuation would not have been seen had not a house been set afire through carelessness. The rear guard under Col. Ebenezer Francis left Fort Independence at about four in the morning.

103

Col. Seth Warner and some Green Mountain Boys were left at Hubbardton to pick up stragglers and press on to Castleton to join the rest.

When the burning house was seen by the British, they roused and rallied to overtake the Americans, arriving about dawn in Hubbardton where British Col. Simon Fraser attacked Warner's troops. Warner fought well, and was about to defeat the British, when a company of Hessians arrived. The Americans took to the woods, losing most of their supplies, many of their men, and their reputation. Everybody blamed everybody, but eventually it was conceded that the defeat was a victory in that it served to slow down the overall march of the British to Albany.

51. Confusion at Manchester — 1777

After the Constitutional Convention at Windsor was adjourned in haste, the Council of twelve men who had just been chosen to govern the new state until elections could be held, after seeing to the safety of their families, convened on July 11 at Manchester. Seth Warner had his headquarters there, having gathered up such troops as he could after the Battle of Hubbardton.

Thomas Chittenden was elected president of the Vermont Council of Safety; Jonas Fay, vice-president; and Ira Allen, secretary. Members were Paul Spooner, Moses Robinson, Nathan Clark, Heman Allen, Jacob Bayley, Joseph Fay, and probably Matthew Lyon and Jeremiah Clark. Benjamin Spencer, originally chosen, defected to the British when Burgoyne sent out his threatening blasts and was replaced by Benjamin Carpenter.

Letters asking for aid from the neighboring states had been dispatched at once. The first official communication from a neighbor to the State of Vermont, by name, came from

Governor Mechech Weare, who wrote on July 19 that New Hamsphire would help. Brig. Gen. John Stark was raising troops to come to the aid of beleaguered Vermont. Stark, however, refused to act under Continental officers. He had retired from the army in irritation, probably justified, when less experienced and younger officers were promoted over him. He attached the condition to his offer of aid that he would make his own decisions, which caused the Continental Congress to censure him, but he was later vindicated.

The great problem with the American troops was the lack of discipline and the multiplicity of commands which resisted each other with venomous infighting. General Schuyler, who commanded the Northern Army, replied in obvious concern that as a New Yorker he could not recognize the State of Vermont, but that he would do what he could in his private capacity. Schuyler and Stark never got along, but they both disliked Gen. Horatio Gates, who soon took the command of the Northern Army away from Schuyler. Gates later led a cabal to oust Washington, which proved to be an unpopular move. Benedict Arnold was angry because Schuyler had chosen Arthur St. Clair to command Fort Ticonderoga. And so the jealousies and intrigues flourished while Burgoyne with his Tories, Hessians, and Indians moved forward, their eyes on the stockpile of supplies at Bennington.

The retreat of the Continental troops from Fort Ticonderga left the entire western frontier of Vermont north of Manchester unprotected. Vermont was filled with unpaid soldiers, homeless refugees, dismayed Loyalists, frantic state officials, quarrelling military officers, bereaved parents, widows, and fatherless children. There were no newpapers, no printing press; inadequate food; the constant threat from Indians; new diseases being spread about by the movement of troops and refugees, with few doctors to care for sick; and only one quasi-lawyer to attend to legal rights, one John Burnham, Jr., of Shaftsbury. How could the new state possibly survive?

52. *Ira Allen Saves the Day — 1777*

A spirit of determination held the new Council of Safety together. Refugees were pouring from their frontier homes ahead of Burgoyne's army. The government was not yet organized. Troops had to be paid, supplies must be procured, and there was no money. The twelve men sat in Manchester in despair, trying to solve the unsolvable.

Thomas Chittenden came up with a generous idea. He had ten head of cattle and his wife had a valuable gold necklace that they could contribute to a treasury. One man after another rose to his feet to offer his goods or to volunteer to raise and pay a company or so of troops.

But Ira Allen, the youngest by far, made the loudest boast of all, that the Council should raise a whole regiment and pay them properly. Hoots of derision were shouted at Ira, and Nathan Clark made a formal motion that Ira Allen be required to come up with the answer of how to raise the money by the time the committee met again the next morning. Half in hopes, half in jest, Ira was given that responsibility.

He was equal to it. When the Council met again the next morning at sunrise, Ira Allen had a solution, one later adopted by the Continental Congress itself. Why not seize the property of Loyalists and use the money from sales or rentals to finance the new State of Vermont? He had spent a sleepless night to hit upon this idea. The delighted Council adopted the measure at once, and Samuel Herrick was appointed the colonel of the new Vermont Regiment. In late July the Council moved to Bennington.

Vermont was seriously undermined by Tories, and no doubt the Council members were glad enough to punish them and raise money at the same time. It was a disheartening fact that some Vermonters had been recruited into the Queen's Loyal Rangers, one of several Tory brigades, commanded by Lt. Col. John Peters of Mooretown, now Bradford. One of the privates in the troop was David Redding, also of Mooretown, who was later hanged as a spy in Bennington — a little-publicized bit of early Vermont history. This group fought at the imminent Battle of Bennington, pitting brother against brother and neighbor against neighbor.

53. The Battle of Bennington — 1777

General Stark and his New Hampshire troops reached Bennington on August 9, 1777. Colonel Warner accompanied him, leaving most of his troops in Manchester under Col. Samuel Safford. The supplies most coveted by Burgoyne were assembled at Bennington, well guarded, and his progress toward Albany had been painfully slow despite the British success at Fort Ticonderoga.

General Stark was well aware of the British plan to cut off New England from the other states by the meeting àt Albany of the army of Burgoyne with the army of Gen. William Howe. Stark's plan was to fight a war of running harassment, especially on the British rear guard, and to frustrate the enemy's efforts to get food.

With 500 German regulars, some Canadians, Tories, and Indians, Hessian Lt. Col. Friedrick Baum was sent to Bennington to capture the American stores. When word reached Stark on August 14 that Americans guarding cattle near North Hoosick, New York, about eight miles from Bennington, had skirmished with Indians, he sent help. It was then that they found that Baum was approaching. Stark immediately took a position which so alarmed Baum that he sent back for reinforcements. On the fifteenth it rained, so only a few skirmishes occurred. On the morning of August 16 many American reinforcements had arrived from neighboring states, including the Reverend Mr. Thomas Allen, the fighting parson from Pittsfield, Massachusetts, who, after praying, took up his gun with the rest.

About three in the afternoon Stark attacked the British. In two hours the British surrendered after a battle "the hottest I ever saw," according to Stark. As soon as the prisoners were collected and the troops were dispersing, and looting, in came strong British reinforcements.

The American panic was brief; Colonel Warner's troops from Manchester had been alerted to join their commander in the nick of time. Again the British and Americans fought. "It was like one continued clap of thunder."

It was here that Stark was supposed to have said, "See here, men! There are the redcoats. Before night they are ours or Molly Stark will be a widow."

The American troops, fresh and eager, fell on the enemy with vigor and continued fighting until sunset when the British again surrendered. The enemy dead, wounded, and captured came to over 900, and a great lot of ammunition and arms were taken.

In Bennington that night there was sadness as well as joy when the wounded and prisoners arrived. Four Bennington men were killed, including John Fay, son of landlord Stephen Fay. The village meeting house was made into a hospital and prison, and every house opened its doors to wounded of both sides. With no proper jail the imprisonment was very difficult, but soon prisoners were marched to Boston. Paul Revere, then in Worcester, Massachusetts, took over at that point of the march.

Enemy losses were many times that of the Americans, and the victory was hailed widely. Congress retracted the mean words about Stark, the man of the hour. Had it not been for the victory at Bennington, the defeat of Burgoyne at Saratoga on October 16, 1777, would not have been possible. There was no more major fighting in Vermont during the Revolution. It is noteworthy that no New York troops took part in the battle.

Two of the captured cannons from the battle are displayed today in front of the State House in Montpelier. They were found discarded at the Washington, D.C., arsenal some hundred years later and brought back to Vermont by Henry Stevens of Barnet, founder of the Vermont Historical Society.

54. The Provisions of the Vermont Constitution

It had been the plan of the Constitutional Convention in July, 1777, in Windsor to hold elections under the new government the following December. The military events of autumn made that impossible, but on December 24 the Council of Safety summoned the convention delegates to meet again at Windsor. (Christmas was not important in those years in New England.)

They had a few more rough spots to clear up in the Constitution, and a new date had to be set for the elections. The first Tuesday in March was chosen for election day, and the sitting of the first assembly would be the second Thursday in March.

Ira Allen had been instructed to have the Constitution printed, but he had not been able to make the trip to Connecticut to the nearest printer. Although Allen in his *History of Vermont* points out that they feared a "discord" if the Constitution was too widely distributed, he did get it printed and at least one copy was sent to each town shortly before the elections in March. Although the document had been adopted unanimously by the duly elected representatives in July, those delegates did not have the authority to ratify it.

Nevertheless, the charge that the Constitution was never ratified by the people is not entirely true. Many of the towns did vote to ratify the Constitution at the next town meeting, and despite Ira's fears, there is no reason to assume that the Constitution did not have a wide reading and discussion in the various towns. Any piece of paper was read and reread and discussed in those days of scarce reading matter.

The Constitution began with a preamble that was not taken from the model from Pennsylvania, as it dealt with the reasons for separating from New York. This was followed by a declaration of rights, including a prohibition on slavery, the first state to so decree. The vote was given to every man over twenty-one who had resided in the state for one year, and every voter was eligible for office. The rights of freedom of speech and assembly and other rights were assured. The second paragraph stated that private property ought to be subservient to public uses.

The legislative power was in one body, but a council of 12 acted as an upper chamber to keep the government running between legislative assemblies. Judges were to be elected by the assembly. In order to keep the Constitution flexible and responsive to the people it was subject to revision every seven years.

On February 6, 1778, Thomas Chittenden proclaimed March 3 to be election day. The constable of each town received and counted the votes for the town representative (two representatives in the case of towns of over 80 people) and then handed to the representative the sealed votes for governor, 12 council members, lieutenant governor, and treasurer, which votes were counted at the meeting of the first Assembly at Windsor on March 12.

Thomas Chittenden was elected Vermont's first governor. As there was no majority, the Assembly voted Col. Joseph Marsh to be lieutenant governor, and Ira Allen was elected treasurer. Thirty-seven towns were represented by 46 men.

They divided the state into two counties, Bennington and Cumberland, each of which was divided into half shires for which special judges were appointed. The lack of courts had plagued the citizens perhaps more than any phase of the unstable government of the past few years.

And the troubles that immediately were loosed on the new Assembly have literally filled books.

55. The First Assembly – 1778

A swarm of problems attacked the new Assembly in March 1778, especially in the matter of the Tory land confiscation. One hundred and sixty-two persons eventually forfeited property, and although the Assembly set up a court of justice for them, it was a difficult situation that divided families and neighbors. Tories were allowed to return to Vermont if they would take an oath of allegiance, but the Assembly also passed acts for the punishment of high treason.

Other Tories went to Canada where, in time, government lands were granted to them. More than 5,000 Loyalist claims were made to the British government in 1783. Some claimed more damages than they deserved, and at least one harassed administrator wrote in distress about the Vermonters who claimed more than they had lost.

It would appear today from available records that the Assembly accorded care and caution, patience and charity toward the Tories, but there was still a spiteful feeling against them. For example, after the Battle of Bennington, when the prisoners were marched through the town, only the Tory soldiers were jeered at and spat upon. The women of the town gladly furnished their bed ropes to tie them up into a gang that was led through the streets.

Another measure to be voted at the Assembly was to send a delegation to Philadelphia to announce to the Congress that Vermont would now like to join the confederation of American states.

One piece of business that was not resolved was the matter of the petition brought to the Assembly by 16 New Hampshire Connecticut Valley towns that wished to be annexed to the new state. Members of the Council recognized uneasily that this was a sort of flattery they were not seeking, for the New Hampshire government would be enraged. So the matter was referred to the people for a vote.

The Governor and Council met in special session in Arlington in April to take care of unfinished business. There was more trouble with the Tories and the defense of the northern frontier. The military needed flour and bandages and ammunition. And Mrs. Lurania McClane wanted a divorce, which was later granted.

The wife of Jeremiah French was misbehaving and causing troubles, as the following correspondence reveals:

"Whereas it has been represented to this Council that the wife of Jeremiah French late of Manchester (now in arms with the Enemy) is very turbulent and Troublesome where she now is, and refuses to obey orders—"

To which the patient and weary Council made this reply: (sic)

"You are herby Commanded to Take said Woman and her children — and Transport them to Head-quarters at Rutland & there diliver them to the commanding officer — to transport them to some convenient place on the East side of Lake Champlain where she can go to the enemy and git to her husband, and also to take of her Moveable Estate — now in her possession two feather beds not exceeding Eight Sheets, six Coverlids or blankets, 5 plates, two platters, two basons, one Quart Cup, & knives and forks if she have such things, her own and her childrens Wearing apparril. The rest — you will sell — and pay to the Treasurer of this State."

56. Ethan Allen Returns – 1778

In 1778 domestic problems in Vermont proliferated while the governing body coped with international intrigue and the elastic boundaries. The internal situation with the Tories continued to be critical.

In 1778 Ethan Allen returned from captivity, raring to do battle for his country. In Newfane, Brattleboro, Vernon, Halifax, and other towns in southern Vermont many citizens were vociferously opposing "the pretended state of Vermont." In late 1777 a convention of these dissenters had met in Brattleboro to appoint an agent to represent them at the New York Legislature. New York responded that she would protect her loyal people, but actually she never did. Even while the newly elected Vermont Assembly was meeting in Windsor in March 1778, the Yorkers were having a convention of their own to write up a protest to "the gentlemen convened at Windsor, under the style of the general assembly of Vermont." They predicted dire consequences for this creation of a new state, but Vermont carried on, even though the Yorker Tories would not admit that Vermont existed.

For instance, in the spring of 1778 in Halifax a justice of the peace with a Vermont commission had one John Kirkley and his wife arrested for assault and battery on the highway to the person of David Williams. The accused were summoned to court, but before the session could get underway 16 Yorkers rushed into the courtroom with bludgeons and attempted to rescue the prisoners, defying the jurisdiction of Vermont, and broke up the court.

When attempts were made to draft Tories into the Vermont militia there were predictably bellicose results. The Yorkers turned around and raised their own company within Vermont for the purpose of fighting Vermont.

In exasperation Governor Chittenden ordered Ethan Allen to raise a hundred men and put a stop to this insubordination. Ethan Allen and 150 old Green Mountain Boys roared into one town after another. The extra 50 men were ones who joined the fun as the march progressed. They arrested 36 Tories and jailed them at Westminster. However, most of them took the oath of allegiance to Vermont and were soon released.

In 1782 Yorkers were still fomenting trouble in Brattleboro. Ethan was again dispatched to quell the rebellion. As he and his men came to Guilford the people seemed very passive, allowing the party to proceed easily through the town. Then, just beyond the village, they found themselves ambushed by 50 Guilfordites. The Allen party broke and fled, but soon they reorganized and began to shout curses in a typical Allen manner at the attackers. Nobody was hurt.

The ringleader of the Yorker-Tory movement was Charles Phelps, who had appealed to Governor George Clinton of New York and to the Congress for help. He was arrested by Vermont in January 1784, and jailed at Bennington. He finally took the oath of allegiance, was freed, and most of his property returned. This was about the last of the Yorker trouble in Vermont.

Ethan Allen, whose first marriage had been an unhappy one, was now a widower and free to marry. In 1784 he married Fanny Buchanan, a pretty young widow. It was a happy marriage, blessed with children. They built a home in Burlington where Ethan was the country squire who wrote essays and farmed. In February 1789, Ethan went to the home of his cousin Ebenezer Allen on South Hero Island to get some hay. Early the next morning, after having had a sociable evening with friends, Ethan was seized with a fit as he and the hired man were driving home. He never regained consciousness and died in his bed on February 12, 1789.

57. The Hanging of David Redding – 1778

In 1778 when Ethan Allen arrived in Bennington, home from captivity in England, he was given a hero's welcome by his friends Governor Chittenden and the Council. The Assembly was meeting in Bennington that June, and Ethan wouldn't have missed it. He visited his cronies at Fay's Tavern where he heard the news that was sweeping the town. There was going to be a public hanging and the people were in a frenzy of excitement.

David Redding had been found guilty of "enemical conduct" for collaborating with the British by selling stolen ammunition from the Bennington supply. He was considered a traitor and a spy and had been sentenced for execution by a six-man jury. People had come from all over to witness Vermont's first public hanging, and then suddenly it was called off.

The people were furious. Obviously Redding was a highly controversial and unpopular man, but John Burnham, Vermont's first lawyer and Redding's counsel, contended that the trial was improper as there should be 12 men on the jury. The excitement was so great that a special guard was put on the prisoner for fear that the mob might lynch him.

But Ethan Allen, who had lost none of his zesty spirit in prison, mounted a stump. Waving his hat, he shouted to get the crowd's attention, and explained the reason for the delay. After all, a hanging had to be legal, didn't it? Go home and wait, he advised, and added with an oath, "You shall see somebody swing at all events, for if Redding is not convicted, then I shall be hanged myself."

This ridiculous remark so amused the crowd that they followed his advice, and a few days later the jury of 12, with Ethan acting as prosecutor, found the prisoner guilty and sentenced him to be hanged.

There are no legal records of the proceedings, or of how the jury was chosen or who sat on it, but the evidence is strong that Redding was tried in a court which had no proper jursidiction over him. Who was this David Redding? Why was he hanged above all Tories? John Spargo, a meticulous historian, says that Redding was a Loyalist and a military spy, not a common thief. He served in the Queen's Loyal Rangers who fought in the Battle of Bennington against the Vermonters.

Since Redding was a military prisoner he should have been tried by a military court. It is believed that he tried to escape but was brought back for the shady trial. Redding never had a chance, and the Vermont government for whatever reason withheld the records.

At two in the afternoon on June 9, 1778, in the presence of an enormous morbid crowd he was executed. He was not given a decent burial, and his body was turned over to Dr. Jonas Fay for medical use. The bones were never buried, and David Redding's ghost is rumored to still haunt the town of Bennington.

58. Vermont's Elastic Boundary

Reading the minutes of the early assemblies is complex at best, but trying to untangle the details of the boundary game that Vermont played with her neighbors is almost beyond comprehension. Here is a chronological run-through of the main events that plagued the Republic of Vermont in regard to her boundaries from March 1778 to February 1782.

In March 1778 when the first legislature met, 16 New Hampshire towns on the Connecticut River petitioned to join the new state, for with the revenue raised by the sale of the confiscated Tory lands, Vermont had no taxes. The Governor and Council were apprehensive about this, but they laid the matter before the people, who voted to accept the towns. Governor Chittenden so notified Gov. Mechech Weare of New Hampshire and sent Ethan Allen, just back from captivity, to Philadelphia to see how Congress would regard this move.

Governor Weare protested so loudly to Governor Chittenden and to Congress, already stirred by New York's fury with Vermont, that at the next meeting of the Assembly in October at Windsor, the New Hampshire towns were voted out. But the towns weren't happy about that. They already had representatives in the Assembly, and they persuaded their Vermont Connecticut Valley neighbors to withdraw with them if Vermont persisted in keeping them out.

By now Seth Warner and his Green Mountain regiment had been sent south with the American forces, and Vermont was highly vulnerable. A British force came up Lake Champlain as far as Fort Ticonderoga, and there was no defense at hand. Middlebury was devastated; prisoners were taken, and there was plundering galore. A union was essential for safety.

In December 1778, Connecticut Valley towns met at Cornish, New Hampshire, at what seemed later to have been a Tory-inspired plot to divide Vermont. The New Hampshire towns decided to take over Vermont. There were rumors that New York and New Hampshire were plotting to split Vermont down the middle, each taking half.

But in February the New Hampshire towns were again voted out. By June, New York, New Hampshire, and even Massachusetts were claiming Vermont, although Massachusetts said she only got in the scrap to keep the others from getting the prize. Congress suggested that the three states make the decision, and angry Vermont was not even consulted.

In November 1780, with Congress taking no stand, 43 New Hampshire towns were voted back into Vermont, and the following January the now strongly united valley towns tried to decide whether to take over Vermont or New Hampshire or both.

Meantime, Vermont, alarmed by Tories and the unprotected Canadian border, got some advice from those consummate politicians, Ethan and Ira Allen. They would persuade the New York towns in the strip between the Hudson River and the Vermont border to petition for admission. This would balance matters. By July 1781 "greater Vermont," stretching from the Hudson River to "Mason's Line" in New Hampshire, was proclaimed.

Congress was mad and scared. Vermont continued her political blackmail until Congress agreed to accept Vermont into the union if she would divest herself of the extra towns.

Cornwallis' surrender at Yorktown took place on October 19, 1781, but the delegates at the convention of 102 towns at Charlestown did not know this when they met on that day. They voted not to accept the offer of Congress; they liked the king-size Vermont.

In December 1781, word was flying about that New York was going to send armed forces to dismember Vermont. Accordingly, Vermont sent across the border troops who glared at the Yorkers for a week until the New York troops, being outnumbered, went home.

George Washington, acting in good faith, wrote to Governor Chittenden urging Vermont to rid herself of the extra territory, upon which the United States would accept Vermont's petition. Chittenden laid the letter before the Assembly, and on February 23, 1782, the Vermont Assembly had the quorum which voted to dissolve the unions and place the borders at the Connecticut River and 20 miles east of the Hudson. The news was taken to Congress, but Congress again refused to admit Vermont.

The Vermont agents came home, tight-lipped and furious. They did not reopen negotiations with Congress, and made no further changes in the borders, leaving them as they are today.

59. The Haldimand Negotiations — 1780 - 1781

One of the most controversial episodes in Vermont's history is the story of the Haldimand Papers. Shortly after his return from prison in England Ethan Allen, one July day in 1780, was stopped on the street in Arlington by a British courier in mufti who handed Ethan a letter and disappeared.

As part of a British conciliation policy, the letter, written four months before by Beverly Robinson, a prominent Virginia Loyalist, came right to the point and suggested that since Congress and the neighboring states were playing foul with Vermont, would she like to return to the fold as a separate government acting directly under the British Crown?

Ethan showed the letter to Governor Chittenden and to his brother Ira. The three decided to keep the matter quiet and do nothing. In August of the same year, General Frederick Haldimand, governor of Canada, got word to Ethan proposing a truce for the exchange of prisoners, and in October 1780, the British moved up Lake Champlain with 1,000 men. Vermont had only 230 men under arms, so Vermonters were understandably nervous. Royalton had just been raided and burned by Indians acting on Canadian instructions.

Justus Sherwood, a Tory British agent and an old friend of the Allens, came in late October bearing a letter to Chittenden. Under a flag of truce he approached Ethan at his encampment at Castleton to confide that Britain was prepared to welcome Vermont into the fold. A truce could be arranged, ostensibly for the exchange of prisoners, and all caution would be exercised — only a month before, Benedict Arnold had been exposed as a traitor. The Assembly, troubled by rumors of treason nevertheless voted for the temporary truce.

At this point, many Tories who had been stripped of their land were welcomed back, a disturbing matter to such patriots as Gen. Jacob Bayley, who hated the Allens and mistrusted this manoeuver. Seth Warner, who was dying, came to see Ethan and asked pointblank if he were dabbling in treason.

This prompted Ethan to send part of his correspondence to Congress. Perhaps that body could be frightened into acting on the matter of Vermont's admission to the union of states. Feeling in the Vermont Assembly was so high against Ethan that a month later impeachment efforts were made against him. Ethan indignantly resigned his commission in the Vermont militia. Was it because as a private citizen he could negotiate better?

However, Ira Allen now took over the secret negotiations. His delaying game succeeded in holding the British to another truce. The end of the affair occurred at Charlestown, New Hampshire, in October 1781, when the expanded Vermont Assembly met. British troops were poised on Lake Champlain, waiting to make a proclamation that Vermont was joining the British when a British scout shot a Vermonter, Sgt. Archaeleus Tupper, by mistake. In a highly unusual manner, the British commander apologized, sending a note by messenger to the Allens at Charlestown, a most suspicious action. How often does a commanding officer "apologize" for killing an enemy soldier?

The messenger, no friend of the Allens, opened and read the letter and stormed into the tavern shouting accusations. Caught red-handed, the conspirators called on Ira, who managed to placate the Assembly by forging a letter and telling some lies.

News was shortly received that Lord Cornwallis had surrendered to the American troops at Yorktown in Virginia on October 19, 1781, so the negotiations were not reopened.

Many people feel that the Allens truly intended to deliver Vermont to the British. Others think it was a piece of masterful but tricky diplomacy to keep the infant state alive by playing off Canada against Congress.

The complete Haldiman papers are to be found in Volume II of Walton's *Governor and Council* for those who would like to make their own decisions.

60. The Republic of Vermont — 1777 - 1791

The surrender of Cornwallis virtually ended the Revolutionary War. Some Tory scrapping continued, but was soon ceased when the Treaty of Paris was signed in September 1783 and ratified by the Congress the following January. The Republic of Vermont found itself in the enviable position of being stronger than the infant United States, with a constitution, no war debts, and a growing population of 30,000.

There was a printing press in Westminster; Judah Spooner and Timothy Green had established it in 1780 and were printing the new state laws and a newspaper, *The Green Mountain Postboy*. By 1783 another printer, Anthony Haswell, had arrived in Bennington; he also did some of the state printing and began a newspaper, *The Vermont Gazette or Freemen's Depository*. In 1784 regular postal service was set up in five towns.

Vermont also began to issue her own money. In April 1781 the Assembly passed legislation for the printing of over 25,000 pounds, redeemable in silver; at the same time a small poll tax and a land tax were voted. Spooner and Green were to print the money, and a law was passed making counterfeiting punishable by death. The printers were soon in desperate trouble, for they found themselves charged with counterfeiting. There were lively doings and investigations in Westminster when the counterfeit bills got into circulation. However, the printers' necks were saved. It was found that incomplete bills had been stolen and finished with forged signatures and numbers and put into circulation by two of the firm's lowly employees who confessed to the crime. Presumably they were not put to death, but the punishment is not recorded.

In 1782 even the Assembly had so little hard money that it could not pay outstanding bills. Reuben Harmon, Jr. of Rupert petitioned in 1785 for leave to make copper coins, and for three years he fashioned coins of ample weight and good workmanship. At this time the other states had not officially issued copper coins. Harmon had a furnace, a rolling machine, and a machine for cutting and stamping so that he could strike 60 coins a minute in a design fixed by a committee from the Assembly.

On one side of the coin was shown a sun rising over mountains and trees with a plough in the field with the words *Vermontensium Res. Publica* and the date 1785 or 1786. The reverse side showed an eye surrounded by 13 stars with the words *Quarta. Decima. Stella.*, signifying that Vermont was the fourteenth star.

The number of coins issued is not known, but it was obviously limited as coined money was so scarce that in some towns not a single copper could be found if a search was made. They were called cents, but they were not the hundredth part of an established unit.

In 1787 Vermont passed an act that goods were acceptable for the payment of taxes and other debts. Vermont got her first, but short-lived, bank in 1803. By that time she had joined the United States and the question of Vermont money had already become history. In 1807 America went on the dollars and cents standard, replacing the shillings and pence of colonial days.

61. Thomas Chittenden — 1703 -1797

What manner of man was Thomas Chittenden, who guided Vermont from a rebellious area of contested land to an independent republic and finally to membership in the Unied States? He was governor from 1777, with the exception of one year, until 1797.

Thomas Chittenden was born in East Guilford, Connecticut, now Madison, on January 6, 1730. His father was a farmer, and when Thomas was 18, seized by wanderlust, he went to sea. His ship was captured and the young man was put ashore on a West Indian island with little money and less prospect of getting home again.

Finally he did get back to Connecticut, with no further desire to travel. He married Elizabeth Meigs and moved to Shaftsbury, Connecticut, near the Massachusetts border. Chittenden represented the town in the colonial assembly, was a justice of the peace, and a colonel in the militia. By 1773 when the French and Indian wars were ended he bought land in the New Hampshire Grants with the Allens, a large tract on the Winooski River, and in June 1774 he moved his family to the frontier.

He was now 44 years old, strong and intelligent. He had ten healthy children, who grew to maturity, and an energetic wife. Until they could build a house they slept on boughs in the open. By 1776, however, they had to vacate as danger from the Indians and from the British in Canada threatened.

Travelling by foot and following marked trees, this remarkable family carried their household goods — the things that could not be buried — on their backs and left their new home for temporary quarters in Danby, which they had to leave in 1777 when Burgoyne appeared. They finally ended up in Arlington where Chittenden was immediately thrust into the critical politics of the moment. Chittenden served in every convention that led up to statehood. When Vermont adopted her Constitution he became president of the Council of Safety to head the government until elections could take place in March 1778.

He was then elected governor and remained in that job until 1789, when Moses Robinson was chosen — something of a political accident, for Chittenden was back in the job a year later. Deeply involved in the Haldimand negotiations, he made some enemies, but history seems sympathetic to his situation. What else could he do with hostile neighbors on all sides and a cold shoulder from the Congress?

Deeply religious, averse to ostentation and flattery, he emerges as a man of rare talents who had the admiration of his contemporaries.

He was a man of no-nonsense. Throughout his years as governor he continued to slop his pigs, serve ale at his tavern, feed the stock, and till the fields. His correspondence with George Washington shows the mutual respect the two had for each other.

Because he lost the sight of one of his eyes he was called "One Eyed Tom," by his affectionate constituents. A legend in his own time, in 1796 he resigned the office he had held for 18 years and died a year later at age 69.

62. Vermont, The Fourteenth State — 1791

By 1787 it was clear that the loose confederation of American states was totally inadequate to govern the country; a constitutional government was essential. Vermonters as usual eagerly followed the news from Philadelphia, where James Madison had engineered a convention to draw up a Constitution for the United States.

In September 1787 the Constitution was signed by most of the delegates and sent to Congress, which submitted it to the states for ratification. On February 4, 1789, the first presidential electors chose George Washington as President and John Adams as Vice President.

Vermont wanted to join the United States, and so did Kentucky. In March 1789, when the first Congress under the Constitution met in New York, shrewd politicians realized that a northern and a southern state should be admitted at the same time for the sake of balance. The door was at last open for Vermont, but there were still a few obstacles.

First there was the matter of settling the old land problems with New York. Vermont and New York each appointed special commissions to work out the claims, and Vermont agreed quite amicably to pay New York the $30,000 she requested. In October 1790 the Vermont Legislature, feeling this was a bargain, directed the state treasurer to pay the sum, thus ending in a gentlemanly fashion the decades of feuding and warfare with her neighbor.

Vermont then called a special election of delegates to see if the people agreed to join the union. After all, Vermont had managed independently since 1777, and there might be objections. The convention met at Bennington on January 6, 1791, and with votes 105 to 2 in favor of joining, formal application was made for admission to the United States.

Then the legislature met in special session and elected Nathaniel Chipman and Lewis Morris agents to Congress. On February 18, 1791, Congress passed an act which declared that on the fourth day of March, 1791, "the said state, by the name and style of the state of Vermont shall be received and admitted into their union, as a new and entire member of the United States of America." The act was passed unanimously and without debate. Governor Chittenden, declared that the Constitution of the United States now became supreme in the new state, superceding local law.

There were no statewide celebrations, but toasts were drunk. In Rutland there was a rally in the town square where an American flag with 15 stars was hoisted. Although Kentucky was not yet in the Union, it was assured that she would be admitted soon, and the flagmaker, whoever it was, decided that a 14 star flag would be wasteful with the fifteenth state on the threshold.

Cannons were fired and 15 toasts were drunk "after a collation" for the leading citizens. A special song was composed, one verse of which, sung by a special choir, sets the tone of the occasion:

Fill, fill your bumpers high,
Let the notes rend the sky,
Free we'll remain,
By that immortal crown
Of glory and renown,
Which our brave heroes won
On blood stained plain.

Stephen Row Bradley of Westminster and Moses Robinson of Bennington were elected the first senators, and Nathaniel Niles and Israel Smith were chosen for the House of Representatives. And the 85,533 citizens of Vermont, now citizens of the United States as well, settled down to a life of relative serenity.

Sects, Anti-slavery & Migrations

63. Iroquois Claims — 1798 - 1952

In 1798 the chiefs representing the Six Nations of the Iroquois appeared in the Vermont Legislature then sitting at Vergennes and asked for compensation for the lands "beginning on the East side of Ticonderoga, from thence to the Great Falls on Otter Creek, and continuing the same course to the height of land that divides the streams between Lake Champlain and the Connecticut River thence to the height of land opposite to 'The Bay,' " nearly one quarter of the state.

Despite the present-day knowledge that the Abnakis of the Algonquin nation also held these lands at various times, as relics and history indicate, the legislature did not deny that this land had at one time been under the domination of the Iroquois.

In 1798, Gov. Isaac Tichenor and the legislature were sympathetic to the Indian cause and made an investigation. They paid the travel expenses of the Indians and gave them a goodwill gift of $100.

But in 1799 Governor Tichenor reported on the investigation and said that the claim could not be recognized because the State of Vermont could not make a treaty without the consent of Congress and that the lands were "granted by the King of Great Britain without reservation of the Indian titles"; that the Iroquois were former subjects of Great Britain and by the Treaty of 1783 the Indian title was extinguished; furthermore, the Indians had been allies of Great Britain.

Substantially, the claim and the response were not very different on the subsequent attempts of the Indians to gain restitution for the disputed land. Although numerous papers dealing with the situation over the years show considerable sympathy for the Indians, they did not win the case.

About 1850 it appears that the claim could have been settled forever by the payment of $89,000, a figure arrived at by the lawyer for the Indians, but the legislature voted it down.

On all occasions the Indian expenses were paid and a gift was given and the verbatum reports of the proceedings in the

Assembly were of a most conciliatory nature.

In 1951 the commissioner, Charles J. Adams, in his findings said he did not feel that any new evidence had been added since 1880 and that the Indians had no case and the matter should be terminated. In 1952 a hearing was scheduled at the Franklin County Court House in St. Albans. Chief Mose Thompson of the St. Regis Tribe, Chief Philip Sagodensta Angus, Chief Sagogete Montour, and Matthew Lazare, secretary of the Iroquois Confederacy, were notified by registered mail, but they did not appear at the stated time. The legal counsel for the Indians was Roland Stevens of White River Junction.

The Indians asked to address the legislature or an appropriate committee, but in the end the claim was denied as in the past.

Historian Lafayette Wilbur in his 1900 *Early History of Vermont* quotes an even earlier historian Nathan Hoskins to say: "The settlers of the town of Clarendon derived their title of lands from the Indians, and this was the only grant obtained from them in the State."

It has been said that "Molly" and "Joe" who died in 1819 at Derby were the last Indian residents of Vermont.

64. Economics and People in Vermont's Early Years

The first 15 years of statehood went well for Vermonters. When the settlers came into the territory and cleared the fields they burned the trees and made potash from the ashes. Land was cheap, and potash was valuable, and clearing would often pay off the land cost in a few years. Ashes were soaked and the water boiled out in the great potash kettles, leaving a black residue in the bottom that merchants would take in trade and send to the ports for shipment to European wool manufacturers who used the ash for wool soap. The year that Vermont became a state — 1791 — 1,000 tons of potash were exported from Vermont.

Energetic Vermonters soon began making potash kettles, for every farm needed one, with factories at Sheldon, Swanton, and Fairhaven among other places. In 1802 a paper mill was begun at Bellows Falls, and that same year Merino sheep were brought to Vermont by William Jarvis, United States minister to Portugal, to his home in Weathersfield.

Sheep raising became popular and profitable. By 1840 there were six sheep for every inhabitant of Vermont, even though world events kept the wool market in an uproar much of the time.

Besides this bounty, wheat and flax grew in abundance, and maple sugar was such a big industry that an incredible 1,000-ton production was estimated for 1791 by historian Dr. Samuel Williams. In 1792 a canal was built at Bellows Falls in the effort to open the Connecticut River for trade.

In 1790 the first United States patent was issued, to a Vermonter, no less. Samuel Hopkins of Pittsford had thought of a better way to make potash. George Washington himself signed the certificate.

The population of Vermont jumped from a little over 85,000 in 1791 to over 154,000 in 1800 despite the terrible roads. Each town was responsible for its roads, but the old military roads supplemented the miserable rutted paths that served as town roads. In about 1800 enterprising people began to build toll turnpikes which especially helped stagecoaches and post riders. There was heavy traffic with Canada on Lake Champlain, and the Montreal to Boston stagecoach served larger Vermont towns.

Ira Allen, who had been on the political front since he was a brash youth, was chiefly responsible for the founding of the University of Vermont in 1791. But before the University could get actually into the business of teaching, Ira went in 1795 to Europe, ostensibly to purchase arms for the Vermont militia.

France and England were at war again. Ira purchased the guns in France, and the ship carrying the cargo was captured by the British. In the ensuing legal battle for the arms, Ira was imprisoned in France and financially ruined. When he came home to live he had to take up residence in Philadelphia, since he would have been jailed for debt had he returned to Vermont, the state that owed its very existence to him. He died, poor and obscure, in 1814.

65. Matthew Lyon — "Seditionist"

Matthew Lyon was an indentured Irish immigrant boy who arrived in New Haven, Connecticut, in 1755 and was sold for a pair of bull oxen to pay the captain for his passage. He settled in Litchfield County, Connecticut, and became friends with the Ethan Allen clan. Naturally, he learned about the new land opening up in the New Hampshire Grants. A keenly intelligent youth, he educated himself and bought his freedom at the age of twenty-one, moving up to the Grants with his neighbor, Thomas Chittenden, just in time to join the Green Mountain Boys in 1770.

He was a party to most of the conventions that led to statehood, fought in the Revolution, and married Chittenden's daughter. In the post-Revolutionary War period he moved to Fairhaven, where with his characteristic imagination and energy he soon owned a furnace, two forges, a paper mill, a saw mill, a grist mill, and a printing office in which he eventually began to publish a newspaper, *The Scourge of Aristocracy*, in whose columns he lambasted the Federalist party of John Adams.

In 1796, Lyon was elected to the United States Congress after several defeats. Once there, he immediately arose and made violent objections to the hifalutin manners of John Adams, making an enormous row about the President's "kingly" attitude. Rep. Roger Griswold of Connecticut sneered at Lyon, whom he considered a crude backwoodsman unfit for Congress, and accused him, wrongfully, of cowardice. True, there had been a misunderstanding between Lyon and old General Horatio Gates about a questionable retreat early in the Revolutionary War, but anybody who knew Lyon would never have doubted his courage.

Lyon spit in the face of Griswold, who then hit Lyon with a cane, to which the Irishman responded with a good clubbing with the fireplace tongs. This fight on the floor of the House of representatives was widely reported, with appropriate cartoons, in the American press.

Lyon continued to write such stinging comments about the Federalists, especially John Adams, that the Alien and Sedition Acts were said to have been passed to silence him, and under their terms he was jailed at Vergennes. These laws, though soon rescinded as unconstitutional, and flagrant prohibitions of freedom of speech and of the press, caused such an outcry that Lyon's case became a national issue. He was re-elected to Congress while still in jail, and was soon bailed out by a company of admirers who carried him off in triumph to his new term in Congress, where he cast the vote that broke the tie between Aaron Burr and Thomas Jefferson for the Presidency.

Lyon's popularity in Vermont was not diminished by his violent opposition to the Federalist party, which was the choice of most Vermonters. He even set up political education societies to spread his beliefs in several towns.

In his later years, Lyon moved to Kentucky and served as congressman from there. At the time of his death he had moved to Arkansas, and, again elected to Congress, he died in 1822 before he could serve.

66. Henry Little's Letter — 1805

After Vermont became a state in 1791, the legislature had no fixed place to meet, and it wandered around from town to town, holding meetings here and there. Every town wanted the honor of having the legislature, so it was 1808 before it was settled that Montpelier would be the capital city.

In the year 1805 the legislature met in Danville, which at that time had only twenty houses in it, including a new inn and a jail. Henry Little was a Danville boy of ten years old when his mother decided to open their house for legislative boarders. Henry was put to work to help.

All the boarders at the Little house were Methodists, according to Henry who, when he was an old man, wrote of this long ago summer. He says: "Our table fare was very good, but it was limited to a less variety of edibles than we now have, there being no cultivated fruit, except a few apples or currants.

"The table ware of the times would be a great curiosity now. Some people ate from wooden bowls, with wooden spoons, but iron and pewter spoons were generally used. Trenchers, or wooden plates, very neatly turned from hard wood, and in size and shape of earthern plates, were much in use, and many people insisted on their use, because they did not dull their knives, which custom required to be very sharp.

"Our boarders had given a few gentle hints that our knives were below standard in regard to sharpness, and finally a more emphatic reminder gave them a keen cutting edge by means of the grindstone. A table bedecked with bright shining pewter plates, platters, basins, porringers, mugs, tea pots, etc., was the highest ambition of many families.

"The broad open fireplace, with blocks of stone or wood . . . was the only means of warming our houses, there being no stoves in that country until some years later . . . Our best floors were covered with clean white sand which was wrought in many fanciful and grotesque figures by the action of the broom in the hands of an expert artist."

Henry Little's letter goes on to talk of punishments. Horse thieves were punished by "publically standing in the pillory and at the whipping post." The pillory held a person by the neck and the wrists, and he would be imprisoned there for the public to see. There were "jokes, jeers, scoffs, and insults, while small boys, for whom there was no law, were active in using unsavory missiles."

But this did not occur very often, said Henry. He even heard that some states cut off the ears or branded people, but not Vermont.

Henry must have been very helpful in clearing the table, making the beds, carrying jugs of hot water for shaving whiskers, carrying the slops, brushing boots, holding horses, and running errands, for when the session was over two of the boarders called Henry and gave him a gift so generous that he never forgot it.

They presented him with a silver coin, valued at six and a half cents. Henry was so overcome that he was not able to get his tongue to work to say thank you, for no boy of his acquaintance had ever had such a gift of money in his life.

During Henry's youth a significant domestic change took place: the introduction of the stove. About 1810 the first heating stoves had come to Vermont, but only for the prosperous. Fireplaces were gradually replaced for heating. The real revolution for women came when the first cook stove was introduced.

According to historian Abby Hemenway, John Conant of Brandon made the first cast iron stoves in the state. The old Conant stove was made for 30 years and served as the prototype for others. When a new stove was brought into a village on a wagon great crowds gathered to see the wonder, and eventually cranes and legged pots and other fireplace cooking equipment were relegated to the barn.

67. Pirates, Smuggling and the War of 1812

In the opening years of the nineteenth century pirates and European powers were seizing American ships and making trade difficult. To avoid war, President Jefferson declared an embargo on trade with England in 1807. When a further embargo was placed on trade with Canada a year later, Vermont suffered, and not in silence. Blatant smuggling was the answer.

No power on earth could have effectively patrolled the Vermont-Canadian border, and Vermont muttered about secession to Canada while the Democratic-Republican party, headed by Jefferson and favoring France, bickered with the conservative Federalists who favored England. Meantime our seamen were being impressed, and more to the point, Vermont could not sell all the goods she had on hand.

In 1808, some customs officers attempted to stop a smugglers' vessel, aptly called the *Black Snake*, on the Winooski River. Two customs men were killed in the fracas. Cyrus Dean, one of the smugglers, was hanged, sentenced by Chief Justice Royall Tyler. Smugglers operated in such numbers that nobody dared attack them. It was during this period that "Smugglers Notch" was openly named as it was on the smugglers' route. There was considerable scofflaw hilarity as smugglers rolled barrels of goods downhill into Canada.

Some towns called up militia groups to train. In the town of Hartland in 1809 sketchy town records show that 200 turned out. Obviously Vermonters were preparing for war since this was repeated in many towns.

President Jefferson managed to defer the war until President James Madison took over, but a Congress dominated by Jefferson's party voted the United States into war in 1812. The people of Vermont were violently against it. With war following the years of the embargo, hard times set in for Vermont.

Lake Champlain was fortified. The first encounter of any consequence was a resounding victory for the British in June 1813, when we lost our vessels, the *Growler* and the *Eagle*. A month later the British destroyed the American barracks at Plattsburgh, and a few shots were exchanged at Burlington. Classes at the University of Vermont were closed and troops and supplies occupied the buildings. There were minor skirmishes on land and lake, and by late summer 1814 the situation was serious.

Green Mountain Boys rallied with no further discussion of party or politics, since the border was indeed vulnerable. On September 11, 1814, 28-year-old Commodore Thomas Macdonough defeated the British fleet on Lake Champlain while land forces fought near Plattsburgh. In a day the British were routed, and there was little more action in Vermont.

The state of Vermont gave Commodore Macdonough a farm overlooking the lake, and in December 1814 the Treaty of Ghent restored peace.

After the peace Vermonters were able to resolve some of the political differences that split her during the disputes between the Federalists and Anti-Federalists. But the scene was not happy for long. Almost at once a series of disasters began to plague the people who were already disturbed by the economic situation. Poverty was so great that it was beyond the people to cope, and the results were to be far-reaching for the fourteenth state.

68. Acts of God, and Poverty — 1816 - 1840

In 1816 a natural phenomenon took place in Vermont that is legendary and unparalleled to this day: there was no summer.

With Vermont already impoverished by the embargo on trade that had lasted for about a decade before and during the War of 1812, the crop failure caused by the weather was a disaster almost impossible for us to imagine today. Spring came early that year, and there were rains until May, followed by a drought until September. On June 8, 1816, just as the crops went in, there was a heavy frost and a foot of snow. The new leaves on the trees as well as all the crops were killed.

The sheep had been sheared and many froze to death despite attempts to wrap their denuded bodies in bags of fleece. There was no month in the entire year without snow — even July and August. The second planting that farmers attempted after the June disaster was just coming up when a severe freeze in September killed it.

There were public and private prayers as livestock perished for lack of food. People survived by sharing with each other and by eating the half-matured potato crop. Seines were thrown into streams for fish. Fish and grains were shipped in from Canada and neighboring states. There is no record of anyone's dying of actual starvation, but there must have been famine-related deaths, for the death toll was abnormally high.

The care of the poor in those days was left to each town. The poverty-stricken families were put "on the town" under the care of the overseer of the poor, so the care for the widows, orphans, old, and infirm varied from town to town. In some communities the overseers were dishonest, hiring out paupers at low wages from which the overseer took his cut. In the town of Dover in 1825 there were three overseers, indicating the size of the welfare problem.

A law often invoked provided that a town could demand that a family "depart the town" if they were paupers who had not lived a year in a town. This was called "warning out." Since the poor were cared for by the town's taxation, it is easy to imagine the lack of charity that often arose towards the unfortunates. The persons who charged least for looking after the old, sick, orphaned, and insane were paid by the towns for their care if the families could not be located or forced into support. Persons capable of working were bound out or indentured under the direction of the town fathers.

Imprisonment for debt was such a problem that some towns allowed the debt prisoners freedom during the day to earn money toward dept repayment.

There were some celebrated persons imprisoned for debt. Judge Chandler, a man of integrity whose wisdom tried to stop the Westminster Massacre, died in prison for debt just a few hours before he was to have been released by special legal action. When Lafayette came to Vermont in 1825 he found his old Revolutionary War comrade Gen. William Barton in the Danville jail for debt. Lafayette was so distressed over this that he immediately bailed out his friend, who had been imprisoned for 13 years. Even Ira Allen was forced to live out his declining years in Pennsylvania to avoid imprisonment for debt. Jailing for debt was an everyday affair until 1850 when legal reforms were made.

In 1817 the legislature recommended an institution for the deaf and dumb; in 1834 Mrs. Anna Marsh of Brattleboro left $10,000 in her will to found a hospital for the insane, the beginning of the Brattleboro Retreat. Charitable organizations and churches took care of many of the poor, but the social conscience that led to reforms in all fields of public welfare was not fully aroused until the anti-slavery societies swept Vermont with moral fervor.

69. The Poorhouse, Schools, and Working Girls — 1830

The poorhouse loomed large in the history of Vermont, almost to the present day. A little verse in Abby Hemenway tells of the low regard for unfortunates:

> Rattle his bones over the stones
> He's only a pauper whom nobody owns.

In the poorhouses, unfortunates of all sorts were lumped in together where dishonest and mean overseers often abused them. Children of paupers could be forced to work. Inmates could be whipped, and often were.

Mary Wilkins Freeman, a social novelist of the nineteenth and early twentieth centuries, spent her girlhood in Brattleboro, and her stories dealing with life in the poorhouse are as convincing as are the statistics about the lot of the poor in Vermont.

In the 1830's parents could give away their children at will, and the employment of children was widespread. Working conditions for children were regulated by the selectmen, if at all, and it was 1867 before a state law required children from eight to fourteen to attend school for at least three months a year and then only if the child had resided in the state for a year. "Humanitarian" laws decreed that no child under ten could be employed in a factory nor could a child under fifteen work more than ten hours a day.

Despite popular notions to the contrary, there were no free tax-supported schools in Vermont before 1864. Towns made such arrangements as they could. In town meetings the selectmen would then, as now, ask the citizens if they would raise such and such an amount for the school. Sometimes no funds were raised, in which case there was no school, or the parents paid privately for education. Most towns did support schools, but attendance was spotty in many places.

Farm girls got a practical education by serving as hired girls. Sometimes these young women were exploited, and being usually poor and sometimes orphaned, they had no place to turn. Marriage was the way out for women as they had no legal status until reformers gradually improved the lot of the female. It is no wonder that young people thought that life must hold something better, somewhere. So they began to depart. As the west opened up, young Vermonters went to lead the way.

Even though Vermont schools were often miserable, enough of them taught the fundamentals that many Vermont girls became school marms. They went west along with

Vermont farm boys who had known nothing but hardship and the value of work, qualities that took them far in a new frontier life. Shortly after the War of 1812, the children and grandchildren of the pioneers who had settled Vermont began a trickle emigration that turned into a flood before the century was over.

70. Canadian Rebellion — 1837

The history of Vermont is closely bound up with Canada. After the American Revolution many Loyalists from Vermont settled in Canada, especially in the area bordering the United States known as Upper Canada or Ontario. During the years leading up to the War of 1812 there was a friendly arrangement among the border people on both sides as they united to hoodwink both governments. Hostility to England continued to be strong in Vermont, and when some Canadians began to grumble against the British government, Vermonters supported them with glee.

The Canadian discontent was a class struggle, with the entrenched Tory establishment resisting the idea of a democratic government of elected officials responsible to the electorate. The Tories disliked the democratic ideas that floated across the border, and they stuffily became even more conservative. In Upper Canada the ruling power was called the "family compact" because Tories were accused of nepotism, giving all the political and financial advantages to their own families.

The Reform Act of 1832 in England gave the middle class the right to elect representatives to Parliament, and this affected Canadian thinking. There were also racial and religious struggles that entered into the unrest in Canada, and the political and social upheaval in Vermont at this time gave a sense of brotherhood in uniting ordinary people against government abuses in both countries. Vermont was still angry over the embargoes of the Jefferson period.

The leader of the Catholic, French-speaking group in the legislative assembly of Lower Canada was Louis Joseph Papineau, who lost support by being too radical. In 1837 the central government passed more restrictive laws, causing a rebellion on November 22, 1837. The rebels were defeated and Papineau fled to Vermont.

In Upper Canada, while the superficial problems seemed to be different, the same basic unrest led to problems between the Anglican establishment and the Methodists. Newspaper editor William Mackenzie was the spokesman for the rebellious groups. A poorly organized rebellion was staged on December 7, 1837, but it was quickly put down and Mackenzie also fled to the United States. He was arrested and briefly imprisoned in New York.

Many rebels came to Swanton, St. Albans, Highgate, and other northern Vermont towns. Papineau held a large assembly at Swanton, and on December 6, 1838, a party of 200 armed Canadians left Swanton to cross over and help the rebels in Upper Canada. Vermont was deeply involved, and so-called "Hunter's Lodges," or sympathy groups, sprang up in the state.

British Loyalists assembled on the Canadian side to repel the rebels, and the invading party was beaten. The rebels then returned to Swanton. The Vermont press openly supported them, but the Canadian government made such loud complaints to Washington that Governor Silas Jennison of Vermont was forced into an unpopular decision. He took firm measure to preserve border neutrality until United States forces took over.

The rebels were caught between the United States troops on one side who would not let them enter the state, and Canadian regulars who pursued them up to the border. The rebels surrendered.

Conditions improved politically for the Canadians after the fracas. In Vermont, Americans who had helped the rebels were arrested but never imprisoned.

In 1840 the British government passed the Act of Union which created the United Province of Canada. Upper and

Lower Canada were now called Canada East. By 1848 self-government in all domestic affairs was granted to Canada, and the rebels were paid compensation for damages sustained in the 1837 rebellion.

71. *Labor Saving Devices — 1778 - 1840*

The first Vermonters built their houses from the logs cut in the clearing of the land. Soon they improved on this with sawed lumber made possible by the many community saw mills that clogged the streams.

The grist mill was so important that towns gave land to millers. At first each farm had its own grain "plumping mill," made from a hollowed-out stump into which a rock was raised and lowered from a limber young sapling. Since this method was wasteful and laborious, central grist mills soon replaced them.

Women's lot improved slowly. Lucky farmwives got water piped into the kitchens by "water rams" which some old Vermonters still remember. A head of water was dammed into the lowest spot of the stream with a tiny opening piped into the dam. The pressure of the water raised the piped stream to the height of the water head, dropped it into a cistern, and gravity allowed it to flow into the house.

Early Vermont women spun and wove the flax and wool from their own fields and flocks in addition to their other staggering list of duties. Imagine the joy when a carding mill opened nearby to prepare the wool for spinning, cutting about a third of the labor. By 1809 there were 135 carding machines in the state, the earliest one reportedly established in 1781 at Bennington where paper, glass, cloth, wool, pottery and gunpowder were also manufactured before 1800. Knit underwear was added in 1802.

The embargoes of the early years of the nineteenth century and the War of 1812 gave great impetus to local manufacture.

By 1809 many Vermont towns were making glass, paper, pig iron, pottery, and had breweries, distilleries, and brick kilns. By 1840 there were 95 factories making woolen goods, not to mention commercial spinning and "fulling," a process that improved the wool. Spinning wheels and home looms began to go to the attic and barn to gather cobwebs.

An important man in the town was the blacksmith. In the days when all farmers used oxen, the blacksmith had an ox frame, a device for lifting oxen off the ground so the smith could reach the animal's feet.

Lemuel Hedge, a blacksmith of Windsor, in 1815 patented a device for ruling blank books and two years later he brought out a revolving ruling machine. A ream of ledger paper could be ruled in twelve minutes. Later he invented an engine for marking mechanics' scales, and also a folding rule and a bandsaw. Unexciting as these things may sound, they saved hours of labor.

Capt. Samuel Morey of Fairlee built the first steamboat to be propelled by paddle wheels and ran it on the Connecticut River between his Fairlee home and Orford, New Hampshire. About 1792 he built a steam-propelled boat only big enough for two and ran against the river current at the rate of two miles an hour. Robert Fulton improved on Morey's invention and got the credit. Morey was bitter about this, and there is a legend that one of his boats lies deliberately sunk in the lake that bears his name. Many poor Vermont inventors had a similar fate for lack of manufacturing capital.

The Gray Power Machine used an animal, usually a horse, to walk a treadmill which provided a take-off power shaft to run various devices. These machines, manufactured in Poultney, were sold in South America until recently. Some people recall washing machines powered by goats on Gray's treadmills.

72. Vermont Inventions — 1796 - 1850

John Cooper of Guildhall moved to Windsor in 1827 with a pump that he thought would work on a steamboat. It did not function very efficiently, but the idea led to improvements that resulted in the founding of the National Hydraulic Pump Co. by Jabez Proctor, father of Senator Redfield Proctor. Jabez Proctor set up the factory in Windsor Prison, used prison labor at twenty-five cents a day, and had his partner Asahel Hubbard appointed warden. This appears to be self-serving, but it worked well in that it gave employment to prisoners and kept prison morale at an all-time high. Hubbard held a later patent on the pump and went to the developing West selling the pumps and keeping the business solvent.

Asahel Hubbard was connected with early rifle manufacture in Windsor. His son-in-law, Nicanor Kendall of Windsor, invented the best sporting arm ever devised, according to some people. The number of machine patents issued to Springfield and Windsor inventors run into the thousands for tools, engines, locks, and devices beyond the imagination of the general public. The towns seemed to attract mechanical wizards.

In the 1830's organs were manufactured in Brattleboro by Jacob Estey, founder of the Estey organ works, and at the same time Thaddeus Fairbanks began the manufacture of scales at St. Johnsbury. Jeremiah Hall of Middlebury originated the circular saw, and soon sawing marble by waterpower was initiated by Isaac Markman of Middlebury.

James Wilson of Bradford made the first globe in America in 1796. Silas Hawes, a blacksmith of Shaftsbury, invented the T square, making the first one from an old saw taken in trade.

Thomas Davenport, a Brandon blacksmith, became fascinated with the subject of electricity. Electromagnetism was a new discovery, and Davenport conceived the idea of making a motor to work with this force. By 1834, he and James Vaughn of Rutland had made several machines which they exhibited in New York. Samuel Morse saw them, and Davenport, who died poor and obscure at the age of 49, always believed that Morse took the idea and gained fame and fortune as an inventor of the telegraph. Davenport invented so many other things that the list fills columns. In 1840, he published a newspaper called *The Magnet*, working the press by electro-magnetism. He originated the notion of moving trains with this force, but somebody else patented the idea before he could raise funds to put it into operation. He also invented the electric piano.

Today there is a marker in Brandon to Thomas Davenport, 1802-1851, "The Inventor of the Electric Motor," placed there long after his death by electrical societies who recognized his genius.

After the Civil War, Vermont newspapers began to carry advertisements for the sale and installation of flush toilets, but the newfangled devices were only for the rich. The term "john" for toilet came into being during the presidency (1825-29) of John Quincy Adams, who had the first water closet installed in the White House. This marvel became known as the "John Quincy," a term that was eventually shortened to "john."

73. Temperance — 1800 - 1850

Liquor was a free-flowing item in the early days of Vermont, when not a house-raising or political rally or gathering of any size could be held without spirits. In fact, it became a dreadful problem. Drunkenness was frowned upon, but a man was not considered drunk as long as he could stand up. When he fell down and yelled for help and clutched the grass for support he was assumed to be intoxicated, not before.

The Council of Censors, the body that recommended constitutional changes, studied the matter in 1806. It was 1850 before a lasting statewide prohibition law came into effect, although by 1820 men were taking voluntary temperance pledges. Horace Greeley, the celebrated newspaper editor from Vermont, was an early temperance advocate.

Local temperance societies began to spring up, and Vermont had a number of charter members in the American Society for the Promotion of Temperance founded in Boston in 1826. Two years later the Vermont Society for the Promotion of Temperance was established and by 1832 there were 200 local temperance clubs. Religious revivals were going on with vigor in these years, and temperance and piety went hand in hand.

In the early days, rum was the most frequently mentioned item in records of merchants. Historian Zadock Thompson says that in 1810 Vermont had 125 distilleries which produced an annual 173,285 gallons which sold at an average of seventy-five cents a gallon and were valued at $129,964. However, by 1840 there were only two distilleries making 3,500 gallons and one brewery making 12,800 gallons. In 1852 manufacture of liquor was entirely prohibited in Vermont, which probably accounts for the popularity of making hard cider on the farm.

Only a few years before, the state had spent for strong drink an annual $1,000,000. A typical town is said to have spent more on alcohol than on the total for all public expenses.

Along with temperance came good works, as temperance societies were often "benevolent" societies as well. Women, a moving force in all this, were allowed membership in the temperance societies and in 1840 were admitted to the anti-slavery societies.

Newspapers were stirred with testimonials and controversies. One Rutland physician, a Dr. Bowen, declared that the blood of a drunkard would "take fire and burn with a bluish flame" and that continued drinking could cause spontaneous combustion in a person.

Episcopal Bishop John Hopkins denounced the temperance societies for he felt such groups were worldly contrivances, not to be confused with true religion, socially valuable as they might be. But most of the clergy lumped all the do-good motives of the first half of the nineteenth century into one pot of morality, often manifested in religious excesses that kept Vermont stirring.

74. Early Religions — 1770 - 1820

Although most of the settlers of pre-revolutionary Vermont were Congregationalists from Connecticut and Massachusetts, they did not all conform to the old Calvinist principles. There is evidence that the settlement of western Vermont was partially motivated by a search for more freedom of religious thought than the settled New England towns permitted. Long before 1800, Ethan Allen repudiated literal scriptures in flagrant writings and speeches that horrified some of his contemporaries but pleased others.

Baptists and Episcopalians, who were not held in high regard in the New England Calvinist towns, worshipped openly in their own way in the new Vermont settlements. The Revolutionary War was a revolution of many ideas, not just political thought. There was a general falling away from the strict organized religion of the Puritans, and the cooperation of the French in the Revolution brought about new tolerance of the Roman Catholics. In fact, in Boston Sam Adams and other leading politicians put a stop to the Pope's Day Riots that had for years taken place on Guy Fawkes' Day, in an effort to reverse the thinking of the English colonists who had feared and hated the French Catholics since the French and Indian Wars.

The Vermont Constitution stated that the Sabbath should be observed. Soon laws were passed to enforce the observance of Sunday and then came an act to support ministers. The towns already had land set aside for church and minister, and many towns taxed the inhabitants to raise money for building meeting houses and supporting the clergy. Some Vermonters objected so strenuously that in 1801 the legislature decreed that any person who did not wish to belong to or support a church could register this with the town clerk by swearing these words: "I do not agree in religious opinion with a majority of the inhabitants of this town."

This was progress in religious freedom, but it was not enough for most free thinkers in Vermont. In 1807 the legislature divested the towns of authority to pass any votes for church building or support and made it no longer necessary to declare religious preference before the town clerk. From this point on citizens were assumed to have total free will in religious matters, with all churches removed from the government's realm.

So Vermonters began to experiment with religions. Among the Congregationalists, Baptists, Methodists, Episcopalians, Universalists, Unitarians, Presbyterians, and even a probable handful of unrecorded Roman Catholics from Canada or Ireland, there arose fanatical sects which began to prosper, especially after the famine and depression of 1816, in response to the terrifying circumstances of life.

About 1800 a religious group called the Dorrilites had appeared in Windham County. The founder was one Dorril, a refugee from Burgoyne's army, who claimed to have supernatural powers so that no man could hurt him. He and his flock were vegetarians who would not even wear clothes that came from animal sources.

This meant no leather shoes, no woolen garments, and a consequent pack of personal problems. One of his followers, a blacksmith, could no longer use leather in bellows, so he made do with linen cloth. They disregarded the laws of the state, their only rules of conduct coming from Dorril who had his instructions from divine revelation, he said.

They had weekly meetings at which the worship took the form of eating and drinking, fiddling and dancing, interspersed with sermons from leader Dorril. They pooled their resources with the treasurer, and the sect attracted many converts and curious lookers-on.

Once after opening the weekly meeting with songs and dancing, Dorril began to speak of his supernatural powers. As usual there were many spectators, and when Dorril began to expound on his doctrine that "no man can hurt my flesh," Captain Ezekial Foster, a giant of a man from Leydon, Massachusetts, rose and struck Dorril down with his fist. A second blow had Dorril begging for mercy.

Foster agreed to stop the pounding if Dorril would renounce his doctrines. Dorril did so, to the astonishment of the congregation, capping it off with the statement that his object had been to see what fools he could make of mankind. There is no record that the people got their money back from the treasurer, but presumably they did for they peaceably returned to their homes and Dorril disappeared.

Another sect that caused considerable comment in religious circles in the early years were the Pilgrims, who flourished in Vermont in 1817. Isaac Bullard, their prophet, who wore a leather girdle and rough garments, entered Vermont from Ascot in Quebec with eight disciples. Arriving at Woodstock he converted a local minister and a farmer and their families. Using their homes as headquarters he increased his following to 40 persons, including a Methodist minister. All holdings went into a common fund, and the word of the prophet was law.

Their chief claim to fame was their affinity for dirt as they said that there was no injunction in the Bible to wash. Zadock Thompson, social commentator who probably knew about them first hand says, "Filthiness they seemed to regard as a virtue; and they were frequently seen, even the adult females, rolling in the dirt of the highway, and presenting a spectacle as indecent and loathesome as can well be imagined."

Bullard controlled the most intimate details of their lives, marrying and unmarrying and dictating by his own whim, which the faithful observed without murmur. Woodstock was relieved when the group departed for Bennington. There they picked up more followers and then moved west with a wagon to carry baggage. By the time they reached Ohio they had over 200 in the group which chiefly subsisted by begging, says Thompson, who adds, "There [in Cincinnati, Ohio] they took boats and proceeded down the river, and a more filthy, lousy, squalid and miserable set of beings the world never saw."

By the time they reached New Madrid, 75 miles below the mouth of the Ohio, many had died or deserted. From there their sect disintegrated, but a few who had come from Vermont returned to the Green Mountains, much chastened by the experience.

75. Religious Sects — 1820 - 1850

The old Calvinist religion of the New England Puritans was centered around an angry God who could alone save mankind, but Dutch theologian Jacobus Arminius, whose thinking influenced the intelligentsia of the day, disputed this. He felt that man could save himself by good works, a philosophy that laid the foundations for the uplift societies that eventually swept over Vermont and the religious movements that cut at the heart of the old religions.

One of the new religious groups were the Universalists, whose founder, John Murray, came to America from England in 1770. Preaching that God was not the author of sin and that men were supposed to succeed on earth, he organized a liberal church that promised salvation to all men, a religion that fitted well into frontier democracy.

In 1837 another new religious sect arose under a Rev. Mr. Bridgeman, a professed Universalist, who astonished the town of Hardwick by interrupting his regular religious services with a sing-song screaming and yelling of passages of scriptures which he claimed was guided by the Holy Spirit. He picked up a few followers, and the New Lights, as they called themselves, attracted so much attention that crowds of people who normally did not attend church came to see the show.

When the congregation got too big for the church they moved to a larger meeting house where members barked in imitation of dogs and foxes, and warbled like birds. Because they jumped and swung their arms and rolled on the floor they became known as Holy Rollers, and when, by divine revelation, the leader said that the men should not shave, they were called Long Beards as well. They were also referred to as the Hardwick Theater, for the town had never had such a show, and it appears that many people of the area preferred visiting the new service to attending their own more staid meetings. The regular clergy, especially the embarrassed Universalists, banded together to put a stop to this and got some of the Holy Rollers imprisoned for disturbing the peace on Sunday. The Holy Rollers did not die out, and as late as the 1930's they were still rolling in the Appalachians.

About the same time that the Holy Rollers came into existence, a Mr. Winchell appeared in Middletown, and it was rumored that he had been involved in counterfeiting, a crime punishable by death. Soon he displayed a divining rod which he claimed would uncover hidden wealth and managed to raise considerable money to finance his treasure hunts, although no money was uncovered for the benefactors. During this time Winchell became acquainted with Nathaniel Wood, a man of equivocal reputation who had a history of radical and unorthodox disputes with the church. These two teamed up to use the divining rod for heavenly revelation, and fanatics flocked around. In an early exhibition of streaking, according to social historian David Ludlum, two young ladies stripped off their clothes on a cold night and fled to the woods because the rod indicated that the devil was in their apparel.

Soon it was revealed that God would send an earthquake to destroy all the unsaved. Despite calling out the militia in Middletown on the stated night, Judgment Day did not arrive. Winchell moved to Palmyra, New York, where he joined the new Mormon movement.

A short-lived but probably the most bizarre of all Vermont religious communities were the Millerites who believed that the second coming was to be between March 1843 and 1844, when the Kingdom of God would be established and the people would be appropriately rewarded. William Miller of Poultney, the founder and leader, reached his calculation of the Judgment Day in 1818 in the wake of the great famine and preached his idea locally, but it was not until 1839 that his theme was picked up by city newspapers and interest in Millerism swept the country.

In 1841 with the end of the world close at hand many Baptists and Methodists took the message to heart. Plans were made for the reception of Christ, and a Castleton woman wove a garment for the Lord. Some people did not bother to plant crops, and many adopted shrouds to wear in readiness for the End. On the fateful day many sat in trees or on hilltops, some with wings attached, and one man injured himself trying to fly.

The home of Ira Young in Jamaica was a center for the Millerites where the faithful gathered on the last days after having disposed of their worldly goods. However, others, who had not become converts, stoned the Young house and tossed hartshorn, the ammonia-scented horns of a buck deer which were roughly the rural version of a stink bomb, into the prayer meeting. Mrs. Young died of a heart attack during the excitement.

Millerism collapsed after the failure of the predicted day of judgment, and its adherents went into other fanatical sects. The 1830's were often called the years of the great revival, for in addition to the upsurge of new sects all the conventional churches were filled with revival zeal. Missionaries, including women, began to pour forth from Vermont. By 1840, at least 45 women from Vermont had accepted the call to places as remote as Samoa, the South Sea Islands, and Indian settlements in the United States.

Probably the best known of Vermont prophets was John Noyes, founder of the Oneida Community, which had its beginning at Putney about 1840. Noyes, an educated man of good family, wrote fully of his theological and social ideas that dealt with spiritual communism and the brotherhood of man and of his beliefs that the second coming had already taken place in a spiritual form at the original Pentecost.

To him this meant that persons were now able to perfect themselves on earth to heavenly holiness. Seeking solutions for human problems, Noyes was deeply involved in the treatment of women; he wanted them to be liberated to be co-equal with men, a doctrine as revolutionary as his famed advocacy of sexual community freedom, which eventually led to his expulsion from Putney to Oneida, New York.

Noyes renounced his United States citizenship and repudiated the Constitution because of the cruelties to Indians and black slaves. Abolitionist William Lloyd Garrison was Noyes' friend, and during Garrison's time in Vermont, when he edited the *Journal of the Times* in Bennington, Noyes urged him to take the same course. Garrison, influenced by Noyes, refused to take his seat in the world Anti-Slavery Convention in London in 1840 because women delegates were excluded.

And so the fervor of religious revival turned into anti-slavery zeal. Vermont did not cease to have periodic religious upheavals over the years, and newspapers throughout the nineteenth century tell of Swedenborgians, the spiritualists, and on and on. About mid-century Roman Catholics began to enter Vermont and become an important religious force.

Mormon founding fathers Joseph Smith and Brigham Young, who were both born in Vermont, were undoubtedly influenced by the religious atmosphere of their childhood. They attracted many of their old friends and neighbors to the westward trek of Mormons, for the 1850 census shows 232 Vermonters living in Mormon Utah.

Vermont's religious revivals continued with less zeal as new issues began to stir the people. One of these involved the Masons, or to be more exact, the anti-Masons, which became a hot political and religious issue in Vermont in the second and third decades of the nineteenth century.

The Masons had been a popular organization among the founders of Vermont, with the Vermont Masonic Lodge founded at Springfield in 1781. Soon four other lodges led to the formation of a Grand Lodge in 1794. By 1828, there were 73 lodges in Vermont.

In 1826 a Mason by the name of William Morgan was denied transfer of membership to a lodge in Batavia, New York. For spite he wrote a book revealing the secrets of Masonry, and an attempt was made to conceal the circulation. The real facts never came out, but it appears that Morgan was kidnapped and allegedly killed by some hot-headed Masons. A wild reaction against Masonry resulted, with the result that Vermont was politically fragmented in the struggle. Churches, especially the Baptists who were growing more powerful, got into the fight. There was a strong current in Vermont, then as now, against élitism and secrecy, and Masons appeared both secret and élite to the working class that was beginning to emerge as the industrial revolution moved into Vermont. Vermont had a number of newspapers by this time, and they played up the kidnap story for all it was worth. By 1827, some Vermont Masons had responded by making public resignations.

The Masons were largely descendants of the original ruling group in the state, which constituted the aristocrats in a sense. Chittenden and the Allens and their crowd were all Masons, and for all the democratic talk, Vermont was founded as a republic with a high concentration of power in the hands of a few.

Anti-Masonry became a political party in 1828 with inflammatory rallies matching religious revivals. Families, towns, and churches were torn apart with a fever that is difficult to understand today. Ambitious politicians took advantage of the situation, and in 1829 the Anti-Masons held a convention in Montpelier and nominated Hemen Allen, nephew of Ethan and Ira, for governor to oppose the National-Republican and the Jacksonian Democrat candidates.

The National-Republican ticket won, but the Anti-Masons got a seat in Congress. By 1832 Vermont Anti-Masons controlled the state, and by 1834 almost all Masonic lodges had ceased operation.

The Whig party gradually absorbed the Anti-Masons and dominated Vermont politics for the next 15 years or so, but the new issue of anti-slavery seized the emotions of the people and provided a cause that superceded all else until its culmination in the Civil War.

76. Politics and Anti-Slavery — 1777 - 1860

The Vermont Constitution of 1777 forbade slavery, the first state to do so, and Vermonters traditionally abhorred the institution, of which they knew little. In 1828 William Lloyd Garrison, the abolitionist, became editor of *The Journal of the Times* in Bennington for a few years, dedicating his paper to fighting slavery and supporting other moral reforms such as temperance, Sabbath observance, peace, and general uplift. Although his Vermont stay was a short one, he managed to get some anti-slavery clubs started, turning the issue into a burning crusade.

By 1840, women were allowed membership in the Anti-Slavery Society, the first recognition of the female as a voting person. There were several organizations with the same general purpose, but some wanted the slaves sent back to Africa and some wanted them to assume United States citizenship. In true Vermont style communities, churches, and families split over the issue.

Orson Murray of Brandon, a controversial do-gooder, kept the movement in an uproar, attacking the people who wanted "colonization" for the blacks. Churches took stands on whether slavery was "a sin" or "an evil."

With the expansion of the West, the problem of whether the new territories would be free or slave had a direct effect on Vermonters. When it was decided that new states could make their own decisions about slavery in drawing up their constitutions, it was important to have enough anti-slavery votes, and many Vermonters who had a footloose urge to go west could combine this with a holy cause by casting a vote for anti-slavery. The movement to Kansas was especially popular in Vermont with emigration societies established to aid the crusade. One company went from Montpelier, two from Rutland, one from Randolph, and in 1855 one from Brattleboro, headed by Mrs. Clarina Howard Nichols, the intrepid editor of the *Windham County Democrat*, who had used her editorial pen to promote the movement during the middle of the nineteenth century. By 1860, 902 Vermonters had moved to Kansas to combat slavery.

If Vermonters had a cause they turned it into a political party. The national Free Soil Party was begun in Vermont as an offshoot of the Democratic party during a disagreement at a Democratic convention at the Pavilion Hotel in Montpelier. The Vermonters refused to go along with the concessions to slavery that the Democrats allowed.

Surprisingly, there was some animosity against the abolitionlists in Vermont. As early as 1835 an anti-slavery meeting in Montpelier, led by the Rev. Samuel May of Boston, turned into a riot in which the speaker's life was in danger until a Quaker woman rescued him by calmly offering her arm and walking him through the angry crowd.

Eventually the northern Democrats, the Free Soilers, the northern Whigs, the Know-Nothings, the remnants of the old Liberty Party, and the Anti-Masons, rallied under one standard in Vermont — anti-slavery — and formed the Vermont Republican Party in 1854.

This was in keeping with the action of Capt. Ebeneazer Allen of the Green Mountain Boys, who set free the slaves taken with the British when the Americans took Mount Defiance in 1777 in the wake of the Battle of Bennington. Captain Allen, a cousin of Ethan, took 50 prisoners including Dinah Mattis, a slave, and her infant child. He gave the woman a written certificate of emancipation and recorded it in Bennington, bearing the heading "Head Quarters Pawlet

28th November, 1777" and Allen's signature.

Politicians forgot their differences briefly in a common disaster when the State House burned. The first State House, built in Montpelier in 1808, had been replaced by a finer granite structure, the pride of the people, in 1836. Among its wonders were comfortable "furnaces" or stoves, but in the horrible cold of January 1857 one was overheated in an effort to warm the rooms for the meeting of the Constitutional revisions committee. The surrounding timbers ignited, and despite the fire pumps, which froze, fire fighters could not stop the flames. Not only was the interior of the building destroyed, but irreplaceable historical papers, gathered by Henry Stevens, were lost. By 1857, using the same granite facade, the present building, modelled after a Grecian temple, was completed.

77. Water Transportation — 1777 - 1850

The Indians and frontiersmen travelled by water in Vermont's earliest days, and water continued to be the chief means of transportation until the middle of the nineteenth century.

Lake Champlain was a busy waterway in the years following the Revolution carrying timber and potash north for shipment to Europe from Canada and bringing manufactured goods back to the frontier. In 1809 the steamship *Vermont* began operation on Lake Champlain, and in 1823 the Champlain Canal opened the lake to the Hudson River and New York City. Two years later when the Erie Canal opened, Vermont vessels could get to Buffalo and beyond.

Lake steamers were a great success for over a hundred years, after the embargoes and the War of 1812 were over. Between 1809 and 1842, for example, 14 lake steamers were built in various towns on Lake Champlain, bringing prosperity to the waterfront. Hundreds of vessels plied the lake. The

Ticonderoga, the last of the steamers, now a part of Shelburne Museum, shows the elegance of the passenger accommodations.

On the other side of the state, efforts at commercial navigation on the Connecticut River began at the same time that Morey was experimenting with steam transportation before 1800. River boats were clumsily dragged through the streets of Bellows Falls then replaced in the water in the early days. In 1802 when a British company completed a canal and locks around the rapids at Bellows Falls, the first navigation canal in the United States, there was an effort to open transportation from the upper Connecticut River to Long Island Sound. Before steamboats could go upstream, "Fall Boats" or rafts were made at White River and Wells River and taken south by rivermen who slept ashore at nights as there were no cabins. The boats were helped forward by poling, and pulled by oxen on the shore through the locks. Usually the rafts were broken up and sold for timber at the southern end of the voyage, so there was brisk business in construction.

When the Connecticut River Co. built the steamer *Barnet* in 1826 there were locks on the river and high hopes there at last the Connecticut and Lake Champlain could one day be linked by canal; but the *Barnet* never even made it to the town after which it was named. The river was too shallow and the locks were too narrow, and all the celebrating that took place on the shores as she slowly inched to her utmost point, Bellows Falls, was for nothing.

Soon the Connecticut was jammed with power mills and dams and the idea of river traffic died, and nobody thought of resurrecting it, for other means of transportation were proving more efficient.

78. Vermont's Roads — 1760 - 1956

The first significant roads in Vermont were the military routes that made settlement possible when the French and English stopped fighting after 1760. Early maps show a maze of roads in Vermont in 1810, but they were only marginally useful trails, covered alternately with mud, snow, or rocks and dust and holes.

The 1779 Assembly passed the first highways act in the state, requiring the selectmen to maintain and survey the roads and to build them when possible. Four days of labor on the roads were required of every able-bodied man between 16 and 60, ministers excused. (A similar law in Massachusetts also excused Harvard students.) Lotteries were held for bridge and road building, but private toll roads and bridges were the best solution to the problems of the intrepid traveller.

In 1785 Col. Enoch Hale built a toll bridge across the Connecticut River at Bellows Falls that was the marvel of the period. Here began the Green Mountain Turnpike, the first of such in Vermont, that ran to Clarendon. Within a few years enough others had been built and connected to form something of a road system in central and southern Vermont. Of course, some people wore "shunpike paths" around the toll gates to the cheat the owners, but the stagecoach routes made them profitable. It was possible to get to Boston, Albany, and Montreal from this turnpike complex, and the taverns along the route dispensed food and drink along with gossip and political news, probably the only joys open to the traveller who suffered over the bumps.

Gradually the towns took over the turnpikes, but the last private one, in Peru, survived until 1917. With the towns in charge, travel remained a risky proposition, and a seasonal blessing at best. Probably the most comfortable means of travel was in a sleigh on a rolled road. Snow rollers, which preceded snow plows, can still be seen here and there in Vermont.

The towns had problems then as they do today in keeping roads up to the satisfaction of the electorate. Dummerston in 1848, for example, had a surveyor of highways, and people were taxed forty cents on the dollar on assessed real estate value for road care. There were many grumbles as the citizens reluctantly paid out from eighty cents to a high of $18.77. Collection troubles were so prevalent that a statute was passed that citizens could be imprisoned until the tax was paid. There is no record of how good the road was.

Persons of that day, and for some years thereafter, could be ordered to repair roads in an emergency and were subject to fines if they did not comply. It was 1892 before Vermont had a road commissioner, and the State Highway Department was established six years later.

There has always been an undercurrent of resistance to road building in Vermont. Many people were set against the Interstates which were first planned in 1946 and begun after the national Highway Act of 1956. Most vocal of all road fights in Vermont was the one concerning the proposed Green Mountain Parkway in 1936.

The Green Mountain Parkway (see also page 214) was to be a great scenic drive over the tops of the Green Mountains, instigated by the National Park Service, the Bureau of Public Roads, and the Vermont Bureau of Public Works. The Vermont House of Representatives turned it down, for the people of the state were enraged at the thought of devastating their Green Mountains for a public parkway, despite the Depression poverty that was bleeding Vermont.

Letters to editors clogged the papers as the issue was fought back and forth from both sides. Governor Charles Smith called a special session of the legislature to reconsider, and the representatives voted to let the people vote, in traditional Vermont style.

The people turned it down in a vote of 42,318 to 30,897. Environmentalists have never been a new or minority commodity in this state.

79. Railroads — 1840 - 1930

Nothing did more to change the face of Vermont than the coming of the railroads. They carried people and goods away and they brought them in, including a whole new element of the population, the railroad workers.

The Vermont Central Railroad was chartered in October 1843, but plans for it had been underway for the previous decade. When the first 27 miles of track, from Bethel to White River, were completed in June, 1848, three cars were run over it. In a little over a year the track was carried to Burlington, losing the race to the newer Rutland and Burlington line which got there a few days earlier.

Railroad openings were causes of hectic celebrations as families came from the outlying countryside to see the iron monsters chug by, provoking women to faint, horses to run away, and men to get drunk with the joy of progress. The Vermont Central held a memorable celebration in Windsor in June 1849, when a train bearing 300 passengers from Burlington arrived at noon. Another train with 1,000 aboard arrived on the Boston and Fitchburg line at four o'clock, and the town spread a great feast for the travellers, with 5,000 people gathered for the fiesta.

Similar scenes took place as a proliferation of railroad companies changed hands, merged, failed, were mismanaged, fought, and seldom got the trains there on time. Everybody who was anybody got free passes, and in the heyday of Vermont's railroads, fortune and fame were made by some railroad presidents, three of whom became governors. There was little cooperation between the lines as an old poem "The Lay of the Lost Traveller" recounts.

With saddened face and battered hat
And eye that told of black despair,
On wooden bench the traveler sat,

Cursing the fate that brought him there.
"Nine hour," he cried, "we've lingered here
With thoughts intent on distant homes,
Waiting for that elusive train,
Which, always coming, never comes;
Till weary, worn, distressed, forlorn,
And paralysed in every function,
I hope in hell, their souls may dwell
Who first invented Essex Junction.

The Champlain Canal had been built in 1820 connecting
Lake Champlain with the Hudson River, and the Erie Canal
two years later led to Buffalo and the West. The railroads
could now supply the transportation link to interior Vermont
whose people ardently wished for this, but the result was
often that it took the people away, leaving ghost villages.

Farmers lucky enough to have the tracks come through
their land profited by having trackside woodlots, for the
woodburning trains ate up wood. That was the day to pray for
strong sons to cut wood. This kind of prosperity made it possible for boys to go to college or the academy in another town.
Sometimes young men worked for their fare by stoking wood
into the firebox for the engineer when they came home from
their factory jobs in Massachusetts or from school.

The 1927 flood wiped out hundreds of miles of track that
were never replaced, taking away such colorful celebrations
as the time in 1849 when the Rutland and Burlington line
offered a free ride to anyone who wished to visit Burlington.
Every inn, tavern, and private house was filled in Burlington
and Winooski, and the fireworks that were set off in every
town where the train passed went down in local histories. No
doubt the conductor was locked in the lavatory and bad boys
pulled the brake cord.

80. Emigration — 1820 - 1880

The troubles and social unrest that beset Vermont in the early and middle nineteenth century, followed by an improved transportation system in the state provided a reason to go and a way to get there, resulting in mass emigration from Vermont. Peopled from the start by the footloose and restless with a pioneering tradition, what could be more likely than to discover in studying population tables that in 1860 nearly half of native Vermonters were living in other states — 175,000 of them, according to the figures.

When Vermont became officially part of the United States in 1791 her population was 85,425, as listed in the census of the year before. Ten years later she had 154,465 people. This tremendous increase kept up until 1820 when there was a sharp drop in the percent of growth. For a half a century the people drained out, although there was never an actual numerical drop in total population in that century.

Why did they go away? For a beginning, consider that the embargo period before and during the War of 1812 put Vermont in a financial slump. Then the year of no summer, 1816, frightened people, who feared it might happen again. The sheep that brought prosperity began to devastate the land, causing erosion that led to floods, and the farming methods of the day took away the humus in the soil, making the land less productive. Then the wool market itself failed.

There were bank failures, hard times, and epidemics. There were less game and fish as more people moved in. The religious movements caused the departure of certain groups. Then there were missionaries who burned with zeal to convert the heathens and get some adventure to boot. Anti-slavery caused the Free Soil movement to Kansas, and Vermont's well-educated girls were in demand as teachers in the South and the West.

With hard times at home the factory wages in New England industrial centers lured young people off the farms. And

163

some went just for the wanderlust of it, especially the 1,100 Vermonters who left in 1850 for the gold fields in California.

By the time the railroads and better turnpikes and canals made travel less horrendous, Vermonters began to escape by the tens of thousands. They went by covered wagon, foot, sleigh, and stage; by barge and boat and raft; by sooty railroad cars where a fortunate few even went in the first "sleepers."

The Civil War left the average Vermont family spiritually and financially close to bankruptcy. The migration continued as families whose sons had not survived the war gave up the old farm and went out to Ohio or Michigan or Kansas to live with the married daughter in a community with a future. Old farm houses were silent except for the mice and squirrels; the barns fell down under the weight of the snow. Whole villages were deserted, and the "Vermont way of life" was spread over America.

Vermonters founded banks and hospitals, colleges, and factories in their new states. They established churches, became senators and governors; the native sons did well. Meantime the population of Vermont did not show a loss (until 1920), but the straight-forward population tables suggest a mystery that brought one cheerful turn of affairs to Vermont while all this emigration took place.

81. French and Irish Arrive — 1830 - 1860

The frantic railroad race in Vermont required laborers, quantities of them, but Vermonters were leaving their homes in such numbers that the labor pool was empty. The 1846 failure of the potato crop in Ireland solved the problem, with results that still influence life in the Green Mountains.

The Irish people of the nineteenth century were angry with the British government and impoverished by their political system. When starvation from the potato blight faced them and they read the advertisements for labor needs in America, they came, pouring into the ports of Boston, New York, and Montreal.

Vermont labor bosses hired some of them at the dockside, and others found their way here when reports of Vermont's green pastures coincided with memories of home. It was cheaper to get passage to Montreal, and some families came by foot through Canada for the beckoning jobs, reminiscent of Vermont's first walk-in settlers. By 1850 there were 15,000 Irish in Vermont.

Previously, the only large groups who came directly from Europe to settle in Vermont were the Presbyterian Scots who had come from Perth and Sterling in Scotland in 1774 and purchased 7,000 acres of land in Ryegate and Barnet in Caledonia County.

The arrival of the Irish in such numbers shook up Vermont considerably, for at the same time an unprecedented number of French Canadians — 14,000 according to the 1850 census — moved into the state, dissatisfied with the English rule in Canada and looking for work. As if that were not enough to change the old regime, sizable numbers of Sicilians came to work on the railroads.

Protestant Vermont was aghast at the influx of Roman Catholics. One of Vermont's more colorful clergymen was Father Jeremiah O'Callaghan, the first resident priest, who came here from Ireland in 1830, chiefly to minister to French Canadians. Controversial Father O'Callaghan, 50 years old when he got here, had in effect been sent by his church for punishment, for he had fought with church authorities on his pet peeve, usury. They probably thought Vermont was a good place for a man rabid on the subject of banks and interest, for banks were few and money was too scarce to be a problem to him in Vermont.

Apparently he got along well with Catholics and Protestants alike. Historian Zadock Thompson asked him to write a history of the Catholics for his *Civil History of Vermont* in 1842, upon which the good father came up with a splendid account of his flock. By 1843, Vermont became a diocese, and Bishop Louis de Goesbriand arrived in Burlington amid blaring bands and a tumultuous welcome by the Catholics. The Protestant press barely noted it, but settled Vermonters accepted the new order with extraordinary decorum, considering their anti-Catholic traditions.

However, some people were not happy to have French and Italian words added to the language nor delighted to have the schools overrun with Irish children. Mostly they feared a foreign voting bloc. About 1850, the insidious Know-Nothing Party with its anti-foreign anti-Catholic platform gained some headway in Vermont. In 1855, some towns managed to elect Know-Nothing delegates to the Council of Censors, for constitutional amendments, but the leading papers of the state, provoked by letters from thoughtful citizens, finally shamed the party out of Vermont.

After the Civil War other European groups came to Vermont, but never in such quantities as the French and Irish who filled the vacancies of the departing Vermonters in the mid-nineteenth century.

82. Underground Railroad — 1830 -1860

Vermonters not only talked anti-slavery, they worked at it by running an "underground railroad" for spiriting slaves to freedom. Slavery was illegal in Canada, and Canadians welcomed the refugees. According to an 1856 Canadian book, *Fugitive Slaves in Canada* by Benjamin Drew, the black population of Upper Canada was 30,000 in 1852.

Because the organization had to be secret there are poor records of how many of these people were taken through Vermont, but presumably a majority of these Canadian settlers were helped by Vermont's Underground Railroad.

Although Vermont had forbidden slavery in her constitution, a 1793 Federal law had provided that runaway slaves could be extradited and returned to their owners. Vermont countered this with an 1840 law that gave a runaway slave captured in Vermont the right to a trail by jury with defense. It was possible under this law to arrest slave hunters for kidnapping, and it was known among professional slave hunters, who were richly rewarded for returning the runaways, that Vermont courts were not going to release slaves to them.

The Vermont Legislature continued to oppose slavery at home and to send repeated petitions against slavery to Congress. Any freed slave was welcomed to Vermont, and fugitive slaves are said to have lived openly here. The 1850 census shows 674 blacks living in Vermont, almost exactly the number, 665, shown in 1970.

There were two trunk lines of the Underground Railroad, one from Bennington up the west side of the Green Mountains and one from Brattleboro up the Connecticut River Valley. Bennington also sent some fugitives to Troy, whence they went north. With the network operating for over 30 years it is impossible to estimate how many people were associated in the system. There are many houses in Vermont today that have bricked chambers around chimneys in the attic or cellar where slaves were warmly lodged as they went from one friendly pair of hands to another. Middlebury, Ferrisburg, Benson, and Barnet all have houses with such hiding spots.

The Quakers were acknowledged to be the founders of the Underground Railroad with "Rokeby," the home of the Robinson family in Ferrisburg, probably the most notable of the stations. Rowland E. Robinson, writer and artist, born at Rokeby in 1833, wrote of his childhood experiences when fugitives were brought in by night and put in a bedroom over the kitchen. The children knew not to ask questions or comment on plates of food that went up the back stairs or the arrivals of wagons in the night.

Ezra Brainerd, who was to become president of Middlebury College, wrote of driving the family carryall across the border with slaves concealed in the hay when he was only a ten-year-old boy.

Wilbur Siebert of Ohio State University compiled material about the Underground Railroad in Vermont in his 1937 book, *Vermont's Anti-Slavery and Underground Railroad Record,* but the emotional flavor of the rescue system is best found in Rowland E. Robinson's classic story "Out of Bondage," which can be found in most Vermont libraries.

83. Slavery and War — 1861

For years prior to the Civil War Vermont had been more involved in anti-slavery activity than any other state, in proportion to its size and population. The South's threat of secession was not an especially controversial matter with Vermonters, for secession had more than once been mentioned in legislative sessions as a possibility for Vermont when members disapproved of federal decisions. Vermont papers indicate little excitement among Vermonters when seven southern states actually seceded from the Union in January 1861 and established the Confederacy in February.

Slavery was another matter. In 1860, Vermonters solidly voted for Republican Abraham Lincoln and his anti-slavery platform, turning away from native son Stephen Douglas, the Democratic nominee. Douglas, born in Brandon, had emigrated to Illinois in 1833 and there contended with Lincoln in the celebrated debates of 1858 concerning "popular sovereignty." Douglas won the Senate seat but lost the presidency.

Washington, D.C., was a slave city, and the government was full of people who disliked Vermont's solid and irreconcilable stand against slavery. Vermonters were outraged when their hero Lincoln, en route to Washington for his inauguration, was a victim of an unsuccessful assassination plot. When Lincoln was passing through Baltimore, the scheme was discovered. The President-elect was put onto another train; and Lincoln arrived unhurt in the Capitol. The

Southerners' reported attempt to seize the government was stopped. The uneasy inauguration took place in March to the relief of the Vermonters.

The Confederate government at Montgomery, Alabama, with Jefferson Davis as its president, had caused little stir in the Green Mountains until the Confederates seized Fort Sumter, a United States fort on an island in Charleston Harbor in South Carolina. Says G. G. Benedict, Vermont's official historian of the Civil War, concerning the year of 1861: "The rumble of the wagons which took 130,000 stands of arms from the United States Arsenal at Springfield, Massachusetts, on their way to Southern depots, had resounded day after day in that city, and no one lifted voice or finger to stop the transfer." Vermont was miserably prepared and astonishingly indifferent to the possibility of war.

Erastus Fairbanks of St. Johnsbury had just taken over as governor when President Lincoln's request arrived on April 14, 1861, asking Vermont for one regiment of 780 volunteers to serve three months with the total of 75,000 troops needed by the United States. Vermont was seriously embarrassed. Nominally there were 22 organized military companies, but all were deficient in numbers and some had no arms. Fifteen years previously the state had repealed the law requiring enrolled militia to do military duty, and the old militia companies who had wildly celebrated "June training day" in the past had almost altogether disbanded.

"Washington is in grave danger. What may we expect from Vermont? A. Lincoln," said the telegram.

Governor Fairbanks, who had only a few weeks before contacted other New England governors about the possibility of a civil war and regional cooperation, called the legislature into immediate session. Within eight days the legislature was in the State House, and when in a burst of patriotism someone suggested that they sing the Star Spangled Banner, nobody knew the words. That evening they hired a Montpelier choir to do it for them while in small towns all over the state men and boys lined up to enlist.

84. Civil War Statistics — 1861 - 1865

Statistics tell a heartbreaking story of Vermont's young men in the Civil War with one in every six soldiers killed, another one in every six disabled.

Of the state's total population of 315,098 in 1860, 60,719 men were subject to military duty. Vermont eventually sent 34,238 men to the war, most of whom were volunteers, the highest proportion of any state. There were few draftees and even fewer hired substitutes. At $300 each, a person could be hired to fill a draftee's place, but so many of them deserted that substitutes had a bad name.

In numbers, 5,124 Vermont soldiers were killed and 5,022 were disabled. Financially, the state was devastated. Five million dollars was raised by the towns, with no expectation of repayment, to supplement army pay and to take care of the families of soldiers. The state's expenses were $9,087,353. In addition, Vermont provided 619 navy and marine volunteers.

As an example, Stowe, a town with about 2,000 total population, furnished 208 men, meaning ten percent of the total population. Of these, 40 died in the war. The town paid out $28,000 which meant $13.50 for each man, woman, and child, a staggering burden in those days of tight money and large families. Twenty-four of the town soldiers were of foreign birth. Clearly, Vermont was dealt a grievous blow even though she was not invaded and physically destroyed as the South was.

The Vermont soldiers called themselves the Green Mountain Boys, and newspapers of the day remarked on their size and "robust bearing." Historians of the period spoke of the bravery and the gallantry of the Vermont troops, as the Confederate historians spoke of the bravery and gallantry of the Confederate troops.

General John W. Phelps of Brattleboro, a West Pointer, was chosen to command the First Vermont Regiment which met in Rutland on May 2, 1861, and left on a 20-car train for Fort

Monroe, Virginia, after a few days of encampment. There was great ceremony and flagwaving, for the soldiers who had mustered for three months duty felt this was an extended "training day" with a summer picnic air about it all.

Soon the troops were involved in bloody fighting in Virginia. Eventually General Phelps led his troops to Louisiana, where he got into an ideological disagreement with General Ben Butler over the rights of slaves. General Butler thought that slaves who turned themselves in to Union Headquarters should be put to work on maintenance and menial jobs. General Phelps declared that they should be trained as soldiers as befit free men. He felt that if the Union officers used the freed slaves as servants General Butler was simply exchanging masters for the slaves.

Accordingly, General Phelps, in keeping with his Vermont anti-slave philosophy, organized the first black troops, at Carrolton, Louisiana, where the camp was thronged with black fugitives. His intention was to raise three African regiments so the Vermont troops could get out of the climate which was killing them like flies.

But ranking General Butler declared that the slaves were contraband and ordered they be used as labor gangs. General Phelps replied that he was going to organize them into troops as he was not willing to become a slaveholder "having no qualification that way."

General Phelps resigned his commission and returned to Vermont, but later the Union army adopted Phelps' policy and asked him to come back. Phelps declined unless his judgment against Butler's stand was totally confirmed. Lincoln refused to "censure" Butler and thereby lost Phelps, a humane and gifted leader of the Union forces.

Butler was so disliked by Southerners that to this day in some places the outhouse or its modern successor is referred to as "the General Butler."

85. Medical Care of Soldiers — 1861 - 1865

Vermont not only gave more than her share in men and money to the Civil War, she sent a high proportion of doctors. Before the war Vermont had three medical schools, at Castleton, Woodstock, and Burlington, giving Vermont enough doctors to accompany her regiments and serve in the Army Medical Bureau as well.

The Army Medical Bureau had inadequate means for taking care of the masses of soldiers who soon needed help for disease and sanitary care as well as wounds. Hospitals were so rare that there was not the slightest chance that they could take care of even a fraction of the needs, and the ones that existed were so dirty that they more often killed than cured, for the necessity of sterile practice had not yet been discovered. Eyewitness accounts of the horrors of battlefields near Washington tell of wounded soldiers of both sides crying for days for water, food, blankets, and help after the first battles.

Early in the war help arose in the name of the Sanitary Commission. Dr. Elisha Harris of Westminster is an unsung hero who was one of the founders of the Sanitary Commission, and its leading sanitarian. For several years before the war Dr. Harris had been prominent in a movement for making clean hospitals and had directed a model floating hospital in New York. After the war he helped found the American Public Health Association.

In May 1861 this Vermonter with some like-minded friends took the train to Washington to see what could be done for the 75,000 recruits who were pouring into the city. Florence Nightingale's work in the Crimean War was uppermost in thier minds, yet they knew the resistance they would encounter from the entrenched Bureau of Medicine. Fortunately, they enlisted the help of Dorothea Dix, who was trying at the same time to get a nursing service started, and together they confronted the bureaucrats who refused at first to take the citizens' committee seriously.

The Sanitary Commission asked for volunteer groups to be established at home to raise money and send supplies, for the government would not provide money. In a few months, however, the government agreed to supply offices, storehouses, and other help of this nature, for it did not take long to realize that recruits who had no place to stay, no decent food, and a complete lack of sanitation could be helped by these volunteers who serviced hospitals as well.

The story of the Sanitary Commission is complex and not very well known, but the Commission is considered the forerunner of the American Red Cross.

In 1862, Governor Fairbanks sent Dr. Edward Phelps of Windsor to investigate the sickness among Vermont troops. A number of good minds went to work on the health of Vermont soldiers, coming up with a plan to bring the Vermont sick and wounded home whenever possible, putting them into three hospitals which the state set up in Brattleboro, Montpelier, and Burlington. When soldiers could not be moved, Vermont had hospital commissioners who visited native sons in hospitals and provided such care as the situation permitted.

Over 1,000 men were brought back to Vermont for care in the first year of the experiment; over 60 percent of them recovered, an astounding figure for the period. Vermont's daring medical experiments during the Civil War were due to such imaginative doctors as Dr. Charles Allen of Rutland, Dr. S. W. Thayer, Jr., of Burlington, and Dr. Henry Janes of Waterbury, who believed that recovery was faster in clean surroundings and that common soldiers deserved the best possible care.

86. Civil War Nurses — 1861 - 1865

When New England's Miss Dorothea Dix went to Washington in April 1861 and offered to set up a Bureau of Nursing, even the hard-nosed Army Medical Bureau listened. Already famous for her work among prisoners and the insane, she was not one to be put off by excuses of men doctors who were horrified at the thought of "ladies" taking part in gruesome warfare.

Nursing was chiefly a home art in protestant New England where hospitals, which had been traditionally run by Catholic sisters in Europe and Canada, were badly lacking. There were no schools of nursing available for Vermont women, so at that time there were no trained nurses here. Nevertheless, the women wanted to serve.

At this moment Vermont's Dr. Elisha Harris went to the New York Infirmary for Women to meet with volunteers to discuss ways of helping the soldiers. This group, the Women's Central Association of Relief, met hostility from the government from the start, but the women, abetted by Dr. Harris, stuck to their primary aim of training some nurses under Dr. Elizabeth Blackwell, America's first woman physician.

Meanwhile Miss Dix, who got herself appointed superintendent of nurses, called for self-sacrifice, earnestness, and high moral standards among her recruits. Nurses had to be mature, unmarried and of "steadfast habits." Not surprisingly some women short-cut Miss Dix's organization and attached themselves individually to doctors or served briefly in hospitals, and departed. Some people regarded nurses as camp followers, and no doubt some were. The amazing thing was that nurses existed at all in the state of prejudice and confusion that surrounded them.

The Sanitary Commission gave support to nurses and cooperated with Miss Dix, who did her best to train women to help the doctors and to keep hospitals as clean as circumstances permitted. Hospitals constantly had to contend with prima donnas and Lady Bountifuls who arrived on charity sprees.

It is estimated that 3,200 women worked as Union Army nurses during the Civil War, but the total number of Vermont women who served is not recorded. In *Our Army Nurses*, compiled by Mary A. Gardner Holland in 1895, four Vermont nurses, Mrs. Fanny H. Titus-Hazen of Vershire, Mrs. Amanda Colburn Farnham Felch of West Glover, and Mrs. Estelle S. Johnson and Lydia A. Wood from "a little country village shut in by the mountains of Vermont" recount their own stories.

The latter two were recruited by Capt. Leonard Stearns, who also enlisted their husbands. In September 1861 the women went to Brattleboro, where they were sworn in with the Fourth Vermont Volunteers in the presence of Governor Fairbanks, who tried to persuade them not to go. However, the women were soon marching with soldiers in a combat area and were assigned to a hospital where Mrs. Wood died of typhoid fever within a few weeks. Mrs. Johnson, who was one of Miss Dix's nurses, stuck it out for almost a year before she returned home.

Amanda Farnham, as she was known in the war, was a young widow with a child who decided to follow her only brother into the service. She left her little son with her parents and enlisted at St. Johnsbury in July 1861 as a member of the Third Vermont Regiment. Amanda Farnham eventually joined Miss Dix's corps and served to the end of the war. Despite Miss Dix and her rigid requirements that nurses should wear shapeless cotton dresses, Nurse Amanda insisted on wearing "full pants buttoning over the tops of her boots, skirts falling a little below the knees, and a jacket with tight sleeves."

Fanny Titus-Hazen managed to join her three brothers in the service despite being declared too young by Miss Dix, who finally accepted her. She, too, served throughout the war.

Many nurses were not paid, but it was finally established that forty cents a day should be provided for the nurses in some hospitals. One of the hardships was having to give up hoop skirts. One nurse said she felt as though she would not be able to stand without the support of her hoops.

There were many unrecorded nurses from Vermont, but the men who wrote the war histories never acknowledged them as part of the war service.

87. Teenagers at War — 1861 - 1865

Countless teenagers enlisted in the war, some falsifying their age and others going with their parents' permission. Boys under 16 sometimes went as official Drummer Boys.

Fourteen-year-old Willie Johnson from St. Johnsbury was a drummer boy of Company D of the Third Regiment. In the seven days of retreat before Richmond, disorganized men threw away equipment so that they would have less to carry. But Willie hung on to his drum and brought it to Harrison's Landing where he was able to drum for the division parade when the troops reassembled, for he was the only drummer who had kept his head and instrument. Willie was so admired for his staunch conduct that he was given a Medal of Honor by the Secretary of War himself for his "high fidelity and pluck."

Another drummer boy, Henry Davenport of Roxbury, was only 11 years old when he went to war with his father, Capt. David Davenport of Company H of the Sixth Regiment. When the father was injured at Lee's Mill in Virginia, and fell in a stream, Henry pulled his father to safety. Returning later for a cup of water for his father, a bullet knocked the cup from the boy's hand, but he survived.

Sixteen-year-old Julian Scott of Johnson, a drummer boy in the same company at the same battle, won a Medal of Honor. Twice he went across the stream to rescue wounded, and later he was in the Battle of Cedar Creek, details of which he never forgot. Julian Scott became an artist of note and in 1874 when still under 30 he painted the spectacular canvas in the State House, "The Vermont Brigade at the Battle of Cedar Creek," viewed by thousands of school children and tourists every year in the Governor's Reception Room. The painting was an instant success, according to the press of the day, with comments in art publications and newspapers in New York and Boston as well as in Vermont. The legislature that had commissioned it was so pleased with the work, which took four years to complete, that they paid him a bonus. Artist Scott had agreed to do the 10- by 20-foot monumental work for $5,000.

Young Private William Scott of Company K, Third Regiment, from Groton, did not survive the war but gained immortality of another sort. Camped near what is now the Chain Bridge near Washington, Scott, who had been two nights without sleep for having covered for a sick comrade, fell asleep at his post. The year was 1861, and the casual army of volunteer soldiers needed more tough discipline, thought some distraught officers. Scott was jailed, tried, and sentenced to death within a few days. Never before had the Army handed down such a sentence.

Hundreds of soldiers of all ranks signed petitions for Scott, who made no effort to excuse himself. On the evening before the execution was to take place a delegation with a petition came to Vermont's L. E. Chittenden, who was on Lincoln's staff, and Chittenden took them directly to the President.

Abraham Lincoln immediately sent a telegram staying the order, using his prerogative for Presidential pardon, but when no reply had been received by ten o'clock that evening Lincoln ordered his carriage and set out in person on the ten-mile drive to the camp to be sure his orders were carried out. In the morning, when the doomed soldier was led out to the firing squad, a proclamation was read to him that ended with the words, "Private William Scott of Company K of the Third Regiment of Vermont volunteers will be released from confinement and returnd to duty."

Civil War historian G. G. Benedict ends the story: "The camp rang with cheers for President Lincoln after the dismissal of the parade, and Scott returned to his company to do good service as a soldier and to give his life seven months later while gallantly charging the rebel rifle pits at Lee's Mill."

177

88. The St. Albans Raid — 1864

Vermont was the only New England state to have a Confederate raid. In the summer of 1864 the Confederate government sent men to neutral Canada to try to arrange the release of prisoners. This effort failed, but there were many Southern sympathizers in Canada who gave aid to Confederates who escaped from Union prisons, just as other Canadians had given aid to runaway slaves. But the Canadian government made it clear that she had no intention of allowing either side to use Canada as a base for staging troops or making war.

Nevertheless, rumors went around Vermont that an invasion from Canada was at least a possibility. When Bennett Young of Kentucky, a Confederate prisoner of war, escaped to Canada he established contact with Confederate undercover agents who arranged for Young and two companions to come by train from Montreal to St. Albans and register at the Tremont House Hotel.

Two other Confederates arrived the same day and went to another hotel, and the next day three others arrived. The visitors lounged around town learning the habits and hours of the people and making note of the locations of banks and livery stables. It is incredible that nobody questioned their presence or turned them in, since *twenty-five* Southerners registered in St. Albans hotels.

Tuesday was market day in St. Albans when farmers brought butter to town to be shipped to Boston in refrigerated railroad cars, making Wednesday the town's dullest day. On Wednesday, October 19, 1864, by prearrangement with his comrades, Bennett Young stepped onto the porch of his hotel and, drawing a revolver declared, "In the name of the Confederate States, I take possession of St. Albans."

Thereupon, the raiders simultaneously forced the townspeople who were on the scene into a huddle on the green, entered the town's three banks, and packed over

$200,000 of loot into a bag. Then they all jumped on horses, which their cohorts had commandeered from the livery stables, and headed for Canada. No bank employees were killed, but a passing stranger who refused to be driven onto the green was shot, and a building contractor at work on a project was mortally wounded by a wild shot, the latter being rumored to be the only Southern sympathizer in town.

Capt. George Conger, a Union officer just home from the service, gave the alarm and led a chase of citizens and home guard across the Canadian border, but the robbers got away. However, they dropped a bundle of money which was retrieved by the posse.

Governor John Gregory Smith, who had a home in St. Albans, was away at Montpelier. A servant girl rushed in to warn Mrs. Smith that the rebels planned to burn down the Governor's house, whereupon, the intrepid Mrs. Smith armed herself and sent a telegram to the Governor which read: "Southern raiders are in town, robbing banks, shooting citizens, and burning houses." The operator then locked the instruments and went to join the people milling around the town, with the result that the frantic governor could get no telegraph response. Excited Vermonters immediately assumed that the town was destroyed and rumors grew wilder by the minute. Volunteers rushed out on horses and trains to aid St. Albans, and Lake Champlain vessels were stopped.

The affair caused serious discord between the United States and Canada for the Canadian government was reluctant to prosecute the captured raiders, and a lengthy international legal squabble developed. The war ended before punishment was meted out, but Canada retrieved and returned only part of the money to the indignant St. Albans banks. What happened to the rest of the money? Presumably the raiders got away with it when they were acquitted and spirited out of Montreal, a scandal that resulted in the dismissal of the Montreal Chief of Police and a reprimand to the Judge of the case.

89. *A Romantic Story*

L. E. Chittenden, chronicler of Vermont, published in 1894 a quaint novel, *An Unknown Heroine*, based on a true story. Union soldier Henry Bedell, a farmer from Westfield in Orleans County, is the hero. Bedell, although exempt from military service due to a dependent wife and children, volunteered in 1862 as a corporal in the Eleventh Vermont Volunteers and soon went to heavy fighting in Virginia.

Meantime, J.L.E. Van Metre, a plantation owner near Berryville, Virginia, had joined the Confederate Army, leaving behind his young wife Betty and an old slave to help her with the farm. When the Confederates and Union troops met in battle near the Van Metre home, Henry Bedell, now a lieutenant, was gravely wounded. Bedell, who had a passion for life, directed his own first aid operations, and when there was a question as to whether to amputate his leg, he demanded that the doctor cut it off if that would save his life.

But the field hospital had to be abandoned, and Bedell, whom nobody expected to survive, was put in the care of an old couple who promised to take care of him with money and supplies furnished by the Army. This part of Virginia was filled with bushwhackers and criminals from both sides, and the treacherous old people spent the money, ate the food, and left the man to die. Bedell in his half-conscious state made up his mind to see the Green Mountains again and forced himself to fight for his life.

But two days later death was upon him when an old Negro man appeared with a bucket of water. After he gave the dying soldier a drink, he disappeared and returned with beautiful Betty Van Metre. Horrified at the inhumanity of the old people, who were still in the house but ignoring the sick man, she berated them vigorously and announced that she would take over the care of this enemy soldier who was, to her kind heart, first of all a human being. Dick Runner, the slave who had discovered the man, and his young mistress stayed by the side of the man until he began to improve. She even enlisted the secret aid of a Southern doctor. When Bedell could be moved, with superhuman effort the old slave and the fragile girl moved him on a stretcher by night to the Van Metre house.

Bedell desperately needed drugs, so intrepid Betty Van Metre drove her wagon through the enemy lines and got supplies and medicines from a Union hospital. Many dramatic incidents later, she secretly managed to transport the soldier under a bale of hay through the lines of both armies and into Washington, where Bedell promised he would now try to get Betty Van Metre's husband out of the Union prison. Betty herself soon contracted a serious fever.

Mrs. Bedell came down from Vermont, and nursed Betty Van Metre through the nearly fatal illness while Bedell harassed the War Department to find Van Metre, whose whereabouts was unknown. With the aid of dreams and prayer and coincidence, the Bedells and Betty Van Metre found Lieutenant Van Metre, unconcious and under a false name, in a prison hospital. He was released and nursed back to health.

The Bedells returned to their Vermont farm and the Van Metres to their plantation. When the war was over the two families remained great friends and visited each other every year.

90. The Fenian Raids — 1866 and 1870

Irish immigrants had a number of societies in America, but the one that most affected Vermont was the Fenian Brotherhood, the American counterpart of the Irish Revolutionary Brotherhood. The Fenian organization flourished among the Irish who fought in the Civil War, and when peace was declared many of them wanted to continue fighting, this time against their old enemy, the British. United States-Canadian relationships had been at a low ebb since the St. Albans Raid, and the general disapproval of Canadian and British sympathy towards the South made the Fenians look to the Canadian border as an ideal place to stage a quarrel with the British Empire.

In May 1866 parties of Fenians began to ride the trains north from Boston and New York, with 300 Fenians led by a Major Spear, a former Union Army officer, arriving in St. Albans on the first of June. Altogether 1,400 Fenians congregated at Swanton, Highgate, St. Albans, and Fairfield. It was evident that something was brewing, but secretly Vermonters, still smarting over the Canada-based Confederate bank robbery, were rather hoping that the Irish would stir up a reprisal against Canada. Vermont Governor Paul Dillingham visited the frontier and decided not to call out the state militia.

Washington, however, viewed it differently. United States Marshal Hugh Henry was instructed to prevent any border crossing and to seize the arms and arrest the leaders. So General Sweeney, the Fenian leader, was arrested at his St. Albans hotel on June 6, adding to the excitement.

Canadian border towns had been deserted by fearful inhabitants when 700 Fenians crossed the border near Franklin, with a few others invading at nearby crossings. The Fenians seized a British flag and one Fenian was killed in the skirmish. Early on June 9 it was decided to abandon the invasion for they were out of ammunition and the British regulars were advancing. Upon returning to St. Albans, the Irish signed paroles and were furnished transportation home. Meantime the town had given a ball for the United States officers who had arrived in town to "preserve neutrality."

In 1870, they did it again. Fenians arrived on the trains and gathered near the border, and once again the United States Marshal tried to dissuade them. When the Fenians decided not to heed his advice, General George Foster, then Marshal, informed the Canadians that he had no troops to stop the

Fenians, but he did arrest General O'Neil, the Fenian leader, and drive him in a carriage to St. Albans. This time the Canadians fought off the invaders, killing a few people, and when the Fenians retreated back into Vermont some of them were arrested, but later pardoned by President Grant.

The Fenian problem was a hotly debated subject in Canada, whose government, like the United States', wanted to avoid an international boundary problem. Both governments soon put troops in the area to prevent further troubles, for a "get tough" policy was necessary. Out of the struggle came some Canadian folk songs, which like many ballads live on when the historical significance is forgotten by new generations.

One goes, to the tune of "Tramp, Tramp, Tramp,"

> Shout, shout, shout, ye loyal Britons!
> Cheer up, let the rabble come;
> For beneath the Union Jack
> We will drive the Fenians back,
> And we'll fight for our beloved Canadian homes.

And another which indicates some Canadian orders not to let things get out of hand:

> But from our brave commander came to us the word to halt
> On no account to cross the line or he would be in fault
> His orders were imperative, actual laws you're not to break
> Nor set foot on Yankee soil a Fenian for us to take.

And the Fenians went home to dream about a lost cause.

91. The Beginning of the Grange — 1871

One of the institutions that developed in post Civil War Vermont was the Grange. After the war agriculture was so depressed in the devastated South that relief had to be provided. At the same time, O. H. Kelley from the U.S. Agriculture Department had the kind of idea that seldom manages to arise and survive in a bureaucracy: he thought it would be a good idea to apply this farm rehabilitation program to bind the wounds of the entire country, stressing that since farmers were all brothers, a secret society or brotherhood encompassing North and South could be the solution for many bitter problems.

Apparently the anti-secret sentiment that had enraged Vermonters during the anti-Mason fight of a few decades before did not extend to the secret proceedings of the Grange, probably because the new group was not an élite establishment but rather was meant for all farmers.

In 1867, the national "Patrons of Husbandry" was established with the local chapters to be known as Granges. Women were given full membership, a daring new idea proposed by Mr. Kelley's niece, Miss Carrie Hall of Boston.

Enterprising Jonathan Lawrence of St. Johnsbury read about this in a Washington newspaper and set about establishing some chapters in Vermont. (In 1790 Lawrence's mother, Deborah Ide, when she was 15 years old, had walked with her sister from Sekonk, Massachusetts, to St. Johnsbury, driving a cow.) On July 4, 1871, the Green Mountain Grange Number One was founded at St. Johnsbury. Soon local Granges were spreading over the state, and within a year the Vermont State Grange was operating, the first in New England, with 13 local chapters as charter members.

The number of local Granges grew so fast that soon there were Pomona Granges, groups that comprised county-wide councils. The Grange became a powerful political and economic force in Vermont, with its own newspaper and cooperative buying groups.

Monopolistic town general stores suffered when the Grange "stores" began cutting into their business. Alarmed merchants even tried, sometimes with success, to join the group and learn the Grange secrets to see if there were some way to stop this heady group of farmers from putting them out of business. The cornucopia symbol seemed to enrage a certain segment of the public who believed that the horn of plenty was not for tillers of the soil.

As early as 1875 Granges were deep into their cooperative ventures of buying everything from organs for the parlor to corn, salt, seed and flour by the barrel. The Vermont Grange bought cooperative machinery and succeeded in directly selling maple products to Grange members all over the country.

The result of this was to make merchants lower their prices. The co-op side of Grange activity gradually died out as more competitive stores were started in rural areas. But socially Granges flourished, and in most towns, where the group took over vacated schools or churches or built new meeting places, Grange Halls were centers of activity. Many a year the memberships of the Vermont Grange ran to 20,000 or more.

Probably nothing was more important than the opportunities the Grange offered to women as the first forum for liberated females. From the start women held office and directed policy right along with the men. They saw to it that the Grange influenced agricultural education, before the days that they had a voice in school affairs, and they promoted ideas of better farming, rural mail delivery, and improved rural roads. The Grange had its own insurance group and credit union, and it supported libraries and Juvenile Granges and other measures that would help farm families.

Today there are about 150 local Granges in Vermont with 8,000 members. It is hard to assess the influence on and contributions to the state provided by the Brothers and Sisters of the Patrons of Husbandry.

92. *From Rocks to Books — 1880 - 1920*

Vermont had always had rich mineral deposits such as slate, talc, iron, lead and even gold, all of which had been extracted in a small way. At the end of the Civil War, with a rising demand for gravestones, memorials, and public buildings, business zoomed when the United States looked to Vermont's extensive marble and granite resources.

The granite used in Vermont's State House had been laboriously hand cut and hauled by oxen, and marble had been mined by hand and wasteful dynamite blasting. Responding to the needs of the time, inventor George Wardwell came up with cutting machines that put marble mining into a new era, especially now that the railroads had usurped the ox team for hauling.

When Col. Redfield Proctor organized a number of small and competing companies into the Vermont Marble Company he set up the largest marble company in the world by 1880. Although the Vermont granite industry for some years led world production it was never established into a single company, but the Barre industries made the town the granite center of the world.

Splendid buildings and works of art brought fortune and publicity to the Vermont stone industry, and an influx of European workers came to Vermont to work in the quarries.

So many people from northern Italy came to work in the granite industry in Barre that in the years between the end of the Civil War and the turn of the century Barre became something of an Italian city.

Spanish, Scottish and smatterings of other nationalities also came to Barre, while the Welsh people mostly headed for the slate quarries west of the Green Mountains. The real United Nations of Vermont was in Proctor, where in 1916, 23 nationalities were represented in the town.

The Proctor family, like other wealthy industrialists of the state, were philanthropists who left a mark on Vermont. Miss

Emily Proctor, whose family had given the Proctor Free Library to the town as a memorial to Arabella Proctor Holden, was deeply and personally involved in seeing that the library was vital to the town. Observing the number of foreign-born children in Proctor, she gathered a large collection of children's books in as many tongues as she could find and had them put on the library shelves for the young newcomers.

Today these rare books are still on the shelves (somewhat guarded, for collectors have tried in vain to buy them from the library) where they are kept for those same children, now old and Americanized, who often come back to look at the books that tided them over during their first few years of life in America.

Even their descendants come, having heard the stories of how Miss Proctor had also sponsored "days" at the library for one nationality after another, where music and food and sociability among the books offered something special in the process of becoming a Vermonter.

93. Some Vermont Philanthropists Before 1900

Vermont's philanthropists have shared their goods with their fellows to a degree that seems out of proportion in a state which is traditionally regarded as poor, homespun, and frugal.

Imagination, as well as wealth, provided the proliferation of hospitals, museums, schools, libraries, and churches that have given Vermont cultural and welfare resources to make other richer states regard her with envy and surprise. Public benefactors in Vermont range from the poor family who sacrificed to give a book to a circulating library, to the magnificent Webb family contribution in the Shelburne Museum. There are the noted good works of the Proctor family and the priceless gifts of Joseph Battell who wanted to see Vermont's outdoors preserved for the future.

A family who used their talents to build a great fortune in Vermont were the Fairbanks of St. Johnsbury. Even considering the flowery prose of the 1890's the Fairbanks shine out from the past as good and charitable people who gave with benevolence and taste. Nineteen-year-old Erastus Fairbanks came to the village of St. Johnsbury in 1811 with his uncle, and later his parents and younger brothers joined him. Brother Thaddeus was shy, introverted, and incredibly bright. Erastus was a businessman who could talk to people, but Thaddeus liked solitary thinking in the back room where he conceived and patented an iron plow when he was barely 30 years old. Next he invented the platform scale, a device that was to make the family rich and change the commerce of the world with accurate measurements. Thaddeus Fairbanks patented 32 widely different items, from refrigeration to cook stoves, in his 90 years of life. His brothers, nephews, and sons worked together in the family business to make it prosper.

The first generation of Fairbanks were poorly educated, but such was their interest in education that they endowed and established schools, not only contributing money but involving themselves as trustees and officials. Erastus was twice governor and his son Horace also held that office. Thaddeus was given so many foreign decorations that locally they called him "Sir" Thaddeus. The next generations, wealthy beyond comprehension in Vermont of that day, had fine educations which they used to fit themselves for service as legislators, ministers, historians, teachers, and librarians. They made grand tours of Europe and used taste in buying works of art to bring home to share.

Sir Thaddeus trained himself to be an architect, and his hand and influence are seen in the "symmetry and beauty of outside appearance" that he says he strove for in anything he made, from scales to factory buildings. Today the visitor to St. Johnsbury can visit the free Athenaeum and Art Gallery where Governor Horace Fairbanks and his family used to greet the townspeople at an annual New Year's Eve reception replete with orchestra and hot house flowers. There two Presidents and even explorer Robert Peary and his dogs were guests among other notables of the day. A block away stands the Fairbanks Museum and Planetarium, where school children have come to be instructed and delighted since 1890. Now supported partially by public funds and donations, it was nevertheless founded in the best Fairbanks personal tradition, a little gem of a museum, built around the family interest in science.

A Vermont museum that was built up with more love than money is Middlebury's Sheldon Museum. In 1875, Henry Sheldon, bachelor town clerk of Middlebury, bought a coin dating from the reign of Diocletian, sparking his excitement in gathering antiques and rare objects that eventually grew into a collection which filled his home and the adjoining barn. When Sheldon died in 1907 he left to the public his collections and his house where today a Board of Trustees manages this expanding museum of old books, furniture, clothes, tools, paintings, and memorabilia of Vermont and the world, all from a farm boy from Salisbury who wanted to share his intellectual excitement with the world.

94. People, Not Statistics — More Post-War Immigration

The band of Scots, who gave Caledonia County its name, came in a body from Europe to Ryegate and Barnet in 1774, but most of Vermont's settlers came from other New England colonies and states over the years.

Yet the 1900 census shows that 44,700 foreign-born people out of a total population of 343,700 were living in Vermont, indicating a new trend. Since the great emigration began in the first quarter of the nineteenth century, the Yankees had been draining out and a new kind of pioneers were taking their places. In 1890, Vermont officially promoted immigration by advertising for Swedish farmers to settle on abandoned farms, a project initiated by an imaginative bureaucrat, Alonzo Valentine.

A committee welcomed the 27 Swedish families who settled in Weston, Vershire, and Wilmington. There were already many Swedes in the stone industry of Vermont, making enough to support Swedish churches in several towns and to make Swedish folk dancing a feature in the Green Mountain State.

Polish people came, too, especially to Bellows Falls to work in the paper mills. One 16-year-old Polish girl, who looked around her native Krakow and heeded the lure of adventure and better opportunities in America, came in 1910 to join relatives in Vermont. Speaking no English, she got a job as a houseworker and then in a woolen mill, all the while learning English in night school. Before long she married a Polish boy, at a suitable wedding where old world dancing and feasting and drinking had a part. In time she moved into one of Bellows Falls' old and typical eighteenth century houses where her college-bred professional children and grandchildren were in and out.

"I never felt any prejudice in Vermont. The Yankees were always so helpful and eager to teach me," she said.

Many Europeans came individually to farm. One boy, who came to Weston from his native Finland by way of Massachusetts in 1910, said that they were so poor when they took over the abandoned farm his father had bought on "Finn Hill" that they lived like the eighteenth century pioneers.

A Spanish woman who came to Montpelier as the bride of a granite operator in 1915 echoed the stories of other European-born citizens of feeling welcomed in Vermont where her descendants became vital citizens.

Several Hungarian families came to Middlebury around 1900, and later in 1957 Vermont was a haven for Hungarian political refugees. That year at St. Michael's College 101

Hungarian scholarship students were enrolled, all young men who had grown up under oppressive political conditions. They were welcomed, with trips to town meetings, the legislature, and homes in the area. Special counselors and teachers and student helpers turned out to instruct them in the English language and American life.

Jews have been among many of the Europeans who have come to Vermont. In Poultney there is a Jewish cemetery whose headstones tell of a long Jewish history in the state, predating Vermont's first Jewish congregation in 1875 in Burlington.

Now German, Italian, Austrian, Swiss, and Scandinavian music, dancing, and accents ring throughout the Green Mountain winter resorts, brought by an influx of ski instructors who have arrived in small but steady numbers since World War II.

All the newcomers have had one thought in common: Vermont reminded them of Poland, Hungary, Italy, Switzerland, Finland, Spain and so on. The Green Mountains were compared with the Alps, the farms were like those of the old country, and the air of freedom was what they were seeking, here or there.

"You see," said one Hungarian man who adopted Vermont, "I never felt that the Yankees regard us as statistics. We're just people to our neighbors."

95. Some Notable Vermonters of the Nineteenth Century

Vermont seems to have had more fascinating people than the population should warrant. Since there is not a town, scarcely a house, it seems, that didn't produce some person of remarkable traits (for good or evil), here follows an account of a few of the people who shaped the times from the Civil War to present.

For instance, there's Abby Hemenway, of Ludlow. Born the fourth of ten children in 1828, she went to Black River Academy where she was a bright student who went into teaching. By 1858, she had brought out an anthology of Vermont poetry whose success gave her the idea of doing something grander, such as writing down and printing everything there was to know about Vermont. Obviously there wouldn't be time enough in a life to do that, so she got local people to write up town histories which she edited into the monumental five volume *Vermont Historical Gazeteer.*

Fire, flood, debt, and theft did not keep her from dedication to her work of research, editing, compiling and writing. Offers of marriage she turned down; there wasn't time for it. She left her Baptist faith to become a Roman Catholic, a daring enough step, which did not cool the ardor of a Methodist minister who wanted to marry her anyhow.

She died in 1890, broken in health and funds, with her last volume not yet printed. Today her history books are as rare, valuable, and fresh as the day she published them.

In a list of books written by early Vermonters the astonishing information appears that George P. Marsh had brought out an Icelandic Grammar in 1838, an unlikely accomplishment for that day! Who was this man? How did he get into such an esoteric subject? George Perkins Marsh, grandson of Joseph Marsh, one of Vermont's founding fathers, is not nearly well enough known in Vermont, although in the last decade he has been recognized as one of the first environmentalists.

Born in 1801 in Woodstock, he was a child who early learned to love and assess the natural world around him as well as to use his remarkable brain as a scholar. Icelandic grammar was only one of his many intellectual pursuits. His general interest in linguistics had led him to the Old Norse language of Iceland. Teacher, lawyer, statesman, writer, artist, diplomat, he left his mark on Vermont, America, and the world.

When Marsh died at his post of Ambassador to Italy in 1882 he bequeathed his greatest monument in *Man and Nature*, a book with the message that man was disturbing nature to a degree that would cause the downfall of man himself. Attacking the American myth of the inexhaustible supplies of the earth, he preached conservation. His book was reissued in paperback by Harvard University Press in 1967, and David Lowenthal, who edited it, has written a thoughtful biography of this great Vermonter.

Here are a few others whose influence shaped the state. There was Justin Morrill, born in Strafford in 1810, who, too poor to afford the college education he yearned for, went to work, educated himself, and became a rich man. He retired in his early forties and went into government, serving for 44 years as U.S. congressman and senator. Although he had significant influence upon public building in Washington, his chief contribution was to education. It was he who created the land grant colleges, making higher education available to all people.

Then there was Col. Joseph Battell of Middlebury, who, in a sense, gave us the Morgan horse by rescuing the strain of Vermont's great breed from certain loss. He privately compiled and published their history and register and gave Vermont the Morgan Horse Farm, where since 1907 the horses have flourished. Battell's great energy and imagination did much more for the outdoors than promote horses; he owned the celebrated Breadloaf Inn where he refused, in the days when automobiles were beginning to bring rich tourists to Vermont, to let anyone arrive at his inn in noisy, polluting vehicles. Horse, carriage, or foot travellers only could come on his land. He was a pioneer in forestry and gave 30,000 acres for training foresters. He was instrumental in setting up hiking trails and was a prime mover in the Green Mountain Club, giving the summit of Camels Hump to the state for mountain climbers. When he died in 1915 at the age of 76, he had left a legacy that has helped make Vermont a haven for lovers of the outdoors.

Also to be noted are: philosopher John Dewey of Burlington, whose writings in education and philosophy changed American schools; Hiram Powers of Woodstock, a sculptor of world renown who made his start by creating figures for a wax works chamber of horrors. When he first saw a marble statue it was as though a bewitching spell compelled him to a new life that led him to Italy where he lived as a sculptor for the rest of his life. Larkin Mead of Brattleboro, another sculptor who gained overnight fame with his snow carving "The Recording Angel," later reproduced in marble. It was he who made the heroic statue of Ethan Allen on the portico of the State House.

There was Henry Stevens of Barnet who founded the Vermont Historical Society in 1838 and charmed everyone around him in his quest for historical documents for and of Vermont, a farmer and innkeeper with a passion for books, who spawned a famous family of bibliophiles. George Jones of Poultney founded the *New York Times*. Horace Greeley of West Haven founded the *New York Tribune*. Mary Wilkins Freeman of Brattleboro wrote short stories and novels that stirred social thinkers. Emma Hart Willard, who lived in Middlebury, believed that women should have as much education as men and founded schools at Middlebury and Troy, New York, to prove it. Lucy Wheelock of Cambridge pioneered in training kindergarten teachers.

A list of notable Vermonters of this period would be incomplete without mentioning that Rudyard Kipling lived from 1892 to 1896 in Brattleboro with his Vermont wife. It was here that he wrote *The Jungle Books* among others, contributed to the *St. Nicholas*, and caused excitement when his English coachman drove the family up Main Street. He left due to a celebrated unpleasantness with his brother-in-law, but Vermont has a substantial claim on one of the most famous literary men of his time who won the Nobel Prize for Literature in 1907.

96. "Snowflake" Bentley — 1865 - 1931

There is a small, enthusiastic clique of people in Vermont who speak with awe of Wilson Alwyn "Snowflake" Bentley, the Jericho farmer who invented a way to photograph snowflakes and measure raindrops that nobody has improved upon since, all the while making discoveries in meteorology and cloud physics far beyond his time.

Bentley, a musical and artistic child, liked to study the snowflakes that fell on the sleeve of his black homespun jacket. Even with the naked eye he could tell that no two snowflakes were alike. He didn't go to school much for the farm was remote and he was frail, but his mother, who had been a teacher, owned books and an encyclopedia which the boy, who gained a reputation for being a bit fey, read with a passion and consequently begged for a microscope.

His parents bought him a magnifying glass and later, with some grumbles from his father he was given a small microscope and a big square box of a camera. Before he was 20, after many errors in his self-taught art, "Snowflake" won his nickname and had rigged up a system for photographing enlarged detailed pictures of snowflakes onto glass plates, pictures of such surprising beauty that some were eventually sold to Tiffany's for jewelry designs and to textile artists.

He made thousands of these glass plates, many of which were made into slide shows for universities and scientific societies, while he contributed to learned journals. In the last days of his life in 1931 his book, *Snow Crystals*, was brought out, replete with plates of the always six-sided snow crystals.

When he was still a young man he discovered a method of photographing and measuring raindrops that has never been surpassed, by simply catching raindrops in a tray of sifted flour and measuring and photographing the resultant pellet of dough.

Although a shy man, Bentley longed to share his delight in these discoveries with his neighbors, who were friendly and tolerant of the genius in their midst but didn't comprehend his passionate pursuits of snowflakes and raindrops. He lovingly arranged a slide show, lecture, and exhibit at his home and sent out invitations so he could explain and infect them with his interest. On the appointed night only six people showed up, to his deep disappointment.

Some of Bentley's glass plates (he used the same camera all his life) are in Vermont colleges and museums, or in the hands of collateral descendants, but most of them were removed to other states when the largely unappreciated, gentle bachelor died in the house in which he was born.

97. Politicians and Heroes—1880 - 1902

Vermont was in the national news in 1881 when native son Vice President Chester Arthur became President upon the assassination of President Garfield. Coincidentally, both Arthur and Garfield had taught school in Pownal.

Chester Arthur was born in Fairfield in 1830, son of a Baptist minister who had emigrated from Ireland. Arthur was a controversial and not very popular president, in a period of great political unrest, and he was not re-elected. He was a handsome man and a dandy dresser, and his valet revealed that the President had 67 suits of clothes and 34 pairs of extra trousers, a noteworthy item that was reported in the press.

In 1896, Gov. William McKinley of Ohio was nominated for President, and his Republican majority in Vermont was so great in the September election that a hundred of the happy voters organized a trip from St. Albans to Canton, Ohio, to congratulate their hero. Newspaper accounts of the affair make dazzling reading in an otherwise dreary political period.

The *Vermonter Magazine* of October 1896 reports: "The cars were handsomely decorated for the occasion. Four portraits of various sizes of McKinley and Hobart [Vice President] ornamented the baggage car. The first sleeping car had a wide banner extending the entire length ... Broad banners covered the other cars containing ringing mottoes..."

There's more. "The St. Albans Glee Club was engaged to accompany the party and contribute to the pleasure and enthusiasm of the occasion ... The inspiring music of the St. Albans Brigade band and the cheers of a thousand people greeted the ears of the Vermont pilgrims as they started ... Each member of the party wore a handsome badge ... each member also carried 'Old Glory.' "

The trains stopped in all towns where bands and fireworks and blazes met them, and there was even a sojourn in a vineyard en route. When the happy crowd reached Ohio they marched to McKinley's home where they presented Mrs. McKinley with a case of Vermont butter moulded in a form of a cross with portraits of McKinley and Hobart imprinted upon it.

During this presentation of the unique gift the chorus sang a song, whose complete words are saved for posterity, entitled "We Want Yer, McKinley, Yes, We Do" to the tune of "I want Yer, ma Honey, yes, I do," the chorus of which goes:

> We want yer, McKinley, yes we want yer mighty bad;
> Ten cents a pound for butter ... well you bet it makes
>   us mad.
> McKinley and Protection
> That is our selection,
> An we want yer, McKinley, Yes we want yer, want yer,
>   want yer
> An we want yer, McKinley, yes we DO.

They made the return trip with more fanfare, well covered and photographed by the Vermont press. The significance of the golden cross of butter is that McKinley's Democratic opponent, William Jennings Bryan, favored free coinage of silver and had in ringing rhetoric declared that the Republi-

197

cans must not crucify mankind on a cross of gold.

When McKinley, a popular and affable man, was assassinated in 1901, his Vice-President Theodore Roosevelt was in Burlington at the Vermont Fish and Game League dinner. When he received the telegram with the tragic news, a special train hurriedly took him to Buffalo, New York, to the wounded McKinley.

In 1902, when he was President, Roosevelt revisited Vermont. He arrived at Windsor on an August morning in a tally-ho coach driven by author Winston Churchill. Theodore Roosevelt made a triumphal tour of the state with speeches, cheering, crowds, bands and banners, making it a memorable holiday.

Probably the greatest celebration Vermont ever knew was when Montpelier's Admiral George Dewey returned an instant hero from his naval success in the Philippines in the Spanish American War in 1899. Thousands of people jammed the railroad stations as the train bearing the Admiral entered Vermont at North Bennington and proceeded to Rutland, Middlebury, Vergennes, Shelburne, and Burlington, arriving at his home city on October 11. Schools were closed, bands played, cannons were fired and bunting covered the towns.

"Dewey Day" was called the greatest day in the history of the state by an enthusiastic press. The Dewey hysteria was not limited to Vermont. There was even a Dewey-for-President movement throughout the country, a bubble that burst quickly, however. During this great delirium Dewey was transported by train and horse carriage, a situation that would soon be missing from public celebrations.

Suffrage, Depression & Conservation

98. Enter the Automobile — 1900

The future of the horse in Vermont was threatened even before Civil War days when a steam-powered buggy was reportedly built in Brattleboro, with enough strength to make a run to Greenfield, Massachusetts. Lack of documentation leaves this machine in the realm of folklore, but a photograph proves that another steam wagon was designed and built by W. A. Lane in Barre in 1900. It could go 15 miles an hour and climb hills carrying heavy loads and was noted for doing the work of three horses at a considerably lower cost. It was totally handmade, even the boiler.

In 1903, the first Vermont Automobile Club was established by 12 owners. Early automobiles seem to have enraged most Vermonters, to the extent that in his 1904 inaugural speech Gov. Charles Bell proclaimed that autos should be restricted to a few trunk lines despite Vermont's 15,000 miles of public "highways." That year the legislature established a registration requirement, and by 1905, there were 270 registered automobiles and motorcycles.

Many tinkerers worked on and even succeeded in making hand wrought automobiles of sorts in the days before mass production of cars. High quality automobiles were manufactured in Bennington in 1919. Karl Martin, a naval aviator, designed, manufactured and sold his own cars which he called the Automobile Wasp, the hit of the 1920 New York Automobile Show. As carefully detailed as a Rolls-Royce, the Wasp was totally handmade with original designing of pointed fenders, wooden steps, mahogany bodies and at least one with a polished aluminum top.

Wealthy "bilists" snapped them up, none of them being sold in Vermont it seems. Douglas Fairbanks had one in which he paraded his wife, "America's Sweetheart" Mary Pickford. Martin's company lasted for six years producing 18 cars in six different models. Karl Martin was one of the now vanished breed of hand-crafted automobile makers, a job description that ceased when the assembly line took over in Detroit.

Vermont's most renowned early automobile venture is the one well covered in Ralph Nading Hill's classic story "Six Thousand Miles in an Automobile Car." Dr. H. Nelson Jackson of Burlington with a companion, Sewell Crocker, and a bulldog mascot made the first transcontinental trip across the northern United States in 1903 for a fifty-dollar bet, an epic journey that makes Ulysses seem like a second rate adventurer. It took over two months to make the 6,000 mile trip over roads that sometimes didn't exist.

Shortly after the intrepid Dr. Jackson got his car to Burlington he was arrested for speeding. He was driving six miles an hour!

99. Outdoor Sports After 1900

The tradition of outdoor sports in Vermont is as old as the Indians who played games summer and winter. From the time Champlain made his visit here in 1609 and reported snow on the mountains in July (highly suspect reporting) travellers, sometimes rich and celebrated, sometimes poor and feckless, have made summer pilgrimages to the Green Mountains.

Of course, those who stayed here the year long learned to survive the winter weather and have a little fun on the side with stave skis, sleds, and skates, but it was after 1900 before outdoor sports, winter and summer, became something of a popular cause in Vermont.

James P. Taylor of Saxtons River who encouraged boys at Vermont Academy to hike, climb, and enjoy the snow, organized the first winter carnival in the United States in 1909. It was he who was largely responsible for the founding of the Green Mountain Club in 1910, an organization that caught the imagination of Vermonters and visitors alike and resulted in the formal establishment of the Long Trail, "a foot-path in the wilderness over the Green Mountains of Vermont from Massachusetts to Canada." Footpaths through the Green Mountains had been around since primitive days, and in more recent times recreational trails had been opened to the summits of Ascutney, Camel's Hump, Equinox, Jay, Haystack, Killington, Mansfield, Lincoln and a few other scenic spots. Mountain climbers, whose list was legion, set about locating, marking, and mapping trails and putting up shelters on them, a tradition that has kept going and growing in Vermont among the hardy set.

In 1907, Dartmouth student Fred Harris built a ski jump in his back yard in Brattleboro. Harris, an outdoor enthusiast, had come home from college full of excitement over the new European skiing craze that was being talked about in cosmopolitan circles. Soon he and his friends built a ski jump in Brattleboro as well as one in Woodstock.

Skiers of the early twentieth century climbed the slopes to slide down again. When news came that sportsmen in Canada had erected a device to pull a person up the hill so that the downward slides came more often and easily, Vermont skiers were intrigued. Woodstock had been a center for winter sports for some years with trains bringing people from Boston and New York to slide, snowshoe, toboggan, and sleigh ride, so it was here in February 1934 that a group of pioneer skiers passed the hat to raise funds to investigate a "ski tow." Clint Gilbert's farm was chosen as the spot and an 1800-foot rope tow, powered by a Model T Ford truck, was built at the cost of $500 The age of miracles was truly here.

Woodstock's rope tow started Vermont on an uphill economic pull that led to the ski industry that has brought people, chalets, new roads, motels, ski shops, wealth, night clubs, the jet set, fun, fights, destruction of some wildlife and remote areas, and headaches for many local officials. However one views it, in 1972 $54,500,000 was spent on Vermont's 71 ski locations with their 209 lifts.

By 1972, snowmobiles, newcomers in the winter sports field, had nearly 33,000 registered machines and enough friends and foes to call for a set of snowmobile laws that passed the legislature that year. In 1973, nearly $19,000,000 was spent on that sport in Vermont.

Camping, canoeing, skiing, snowmobiling, hiking, climbing, ice-fishing, hunting, bird watching, or hauling buckets of maple sap, Vermont's outdoors has had something for everybody.

100. Aviation in Vermont — Early 1900's

Fred Harris of Brattleboro, who pioneered in skiing, was an early aviator as well. Writing in an old *Vermonter Magazine*, he says that he and Lieutenant P. D. Lucas made the first air trip from New York to Vermont. However, flying already had a respectable history in Vermont by that time.

Before airplanes appeared in Vermont skies, balloons were on the scene. Nason Arnold of Brattleboro held one of the earliest licenses in the Aero Club of America and in 1908 took part in the international balloon races in Germany.

The Wright Brothers and their experiments at Kitty Hawk captured the minds of boys everywhere. George Schmitt of Rutland, like many youths of the times, read everything he could get his hands on concerning aviation, and in 1909 when he was 18 years old he built a glider and launched it successfully at his home on the south side of Rutland. In 1910, the young man bought an airplane and taught himself to fly. Schmitt's short life was an adventure of early aviation history before he became Vermont's first air fatality in 1913 at Rutland.

Another Vermont glider prodigy was Charles Hampson Grant of Peru, who launched his first handmade glider in 1909. Grant's glider crashed on takeoff, but undaunted he built another which flew successfully in 1910. Made of muslin, wire, and light wood it sailed 70 feet from the roof of his house. Young Grant made more and better gliders, and in time became a distinguished aeronautical engineer, inventor, and writer.

The first sustained heavier than air flight in Vermont took place at the Caledonia State Fair in September 1910 when Charles Willard took off from the oval race track and flew in a Curtiss bi-plane for six minutes, giving the crowd of spectators the literal thrill of a lifetime. For this remarkable stunt he was paid $1,000.

Ten thousand people came by car, train, wagon, and on foot to see the highly advertised miracle. Willard and his plane came by train, and he assembled the light machine in a tent set up for the purpose. The pilot sat exposed in the front of the 32 foot plane with its bamboo outriggers and a 50 horse power motor. Like many other barnstormers Willard played the fairground circuits, where most of the people of the day got their first sight of man in flight.

Irah Spaulding of Brattleboro was probably the first Vermonter to hold a pilot's license, which he earned in California, but the man who did the first and the most for Vermont aviation in early years was Governor James Hartness.

Hartness was a bright boy who turned his talents to mechanics. When he was 28 years old, a veteran of ten years in machine shops, he moved to Springfield as a shop superintendent. Machine shops were creating new parts for new inventions, such as automobiles, in those days. A man who never stopped investigating things, James Hartness in 1916 at age 55 learned to fly and received his amateur pilot's license. By the time he was elected governor in 1921 he had established Vermont's first airfield and flying school at Springfield, as well as founding the Aero Club of Vermont.

When in 1927 the world was mad with excitement over the universal hero, Charles Lindburgh, Vermont was ready for him. On July 27 Lindy, the Lone Eagle, flew into Vermont to be met by the flying governor.

101. War and Women — Before and After
1917

Vermont had a regiment ready to go when the call came for troops in 1917 as America entered World War I including a number of aviators, 18 of whom were killed. Sixteen thousand Vermont men took part, and when women stepped into the jobs vacated by the men, the question of women's suffrage, which had been at a low steady rumble in Vermont for nearly a century, became a loud roar.

A recap of the women's rights question shows slow steps forward since 1840 when women were admitted as voting members by the Vermont Anti-Slavery Society. Following this example, in the 1850's some of the temperance societies also accepted women. From 1843 to 1853 women found a sparkling champion in Clarina Howard Nichols who edited Brattleboro's *Windham County Democrat*, where editorially she campaigned for rights of women, including the right to vote. In 1852, the intrepid Mrs. Nichols addressed the legislature (unheard of!) and carried a petition for the right of women to vote in district school meetings. This was not granted until 1880, but she made history, and caused a lot of comment, pro and con, in the newspapers of the period.

After the Civil War and the formation of the national Woman Suffrage Association, there was a flurry of demands for suffrage in Vermont. Spirited meetings were held with such famous speakers as Mary Livermore, who addressed a rally in Montpelier. In June, 1870, 25 women of St. Johnsbury signed a petition to the legislature asking for the vote. The Council of Censors actually proposed a constitutional change to accomplish this, but it was violently opposed and did not pass. However, it was some consolation that the newly formed Grange admitted women as full voting members.

By 1875, women were not only admitted to the University of Vermont but had two graduates. Carrie Burnham of

Craftsbury led the nation to become America's first woman lawyer, graduating from the University of Pennsylvania Law School in 1883 after years of struggles for admission. Carrie Burnham married Philadelphia lawyer Damon Kilgore and had two daughters as well as carrying on a distinguished law practice. It was in character that she was the first American woman to go aloft in a balloon. She is buried in Craftsbury.

In 1906, the legislature made women eligible for offices of town clerk and treasurer and library and school director, but they still could not vote in town meeting.

When Congress passed the Nineteenth Amendment to allow women to vote, ratification was needed by three-fourths of the states. Finally, with only one more state's legislative affirmation required, Vermont women petitioned Gov. Percival Clement to call an extra session of the legislature so Vermont could carry the amendment. Governor Clement refused, and it seemed that the Vermont women would not have a chance to vote in the 1920 election. Tennessee came through with the necessary ratification and Vermont women at last had the vote in 1920, from town meetings to national elections.

How many women voted? Nobody seems to know, but historian Walter Crockett says that "many women voted for Mr. Hartness," who was elected governor.

It is apparent that the Vermont historians of the day did not consider the woman vote noteworthy. Arthur Stone does not mention it at all, but instead devotes a chapter in his 1,000-page history to "The Feminine Movement," a run-through of women's (non-political) clubs of the period in Vermont. Crockett devotes two pages to women's suffrage in his *History of Vermont*, mostly a repeat of the governor's speech of why he would not call the legislature into special session when the women petitioned.

In 1921, Edna Beard of Orange became the first woman legislator, and there has been no session without women since. In 1953, when Consuelo Bailey became the first woman in the nation to become a state Speaker of the House, *Life* magazine ran a full page feature on Vermont's 52 women legislators of that year. In 1955, Mrs. Bailey became the nation's first female Lieutenant Governor.

102. Vermont's First Radio Station — 1922

When Charles Doe of Bellows Falls was a youngster in Milton, Massachusetts, in 1915, his father and uncle were radio buffs. Those were the days when Marconi was celebrated in the press for broadcasting and receiving messages through the air waves, and around Boston there were many people experimenting with this fascinating new hobby. It was a natural step for young Doe to join the Navy in 1916 on the eve of World War I and be assigned to the new Naval Radio School at Harvard. He already knew a lot about radio, and he learned a lot more which he recorded in his meticulous notebook.

After graduating from this pioneer school, Radioman Second Class Doe served on a troop ship that took him to France. They communicated with other ships by means of a transmitter that spoke in tapped-out code. Back home again, Doe bought a motorcycle in 1917 and in typical sailor-on-a-motorcycle style, he roared from Boston to Bellows Falls to see a friend.

When the war was over, after working at Harvard Medical School on radio experiments, he couldn't get Vermont out of his mind. The year was 1921; Doe had a second class commercial license; and there was no radio station in Vermont. Would radio expert Doe like to come to Bellows Falls and set up a station for the (now defunct) Vermont Farm Machinery Co.? Charles Doe would. An imaginative official at the flourishing factory felt that the time had come for Vermont farmers to take advantage of radio, the miracle of the age.

Young Doe was given a free hand to set up Vermont's first FCC licensed ratio station, WLAK, a 500-watt, 2500-volt, D.C., broadcasting outfit. On September 4, 1922, it had its debut, featuring Bellows Falls' own, her favorite Brazil's Orchestra. The Farm Machinery Company would sell radio receiving kits to farmers and provide a broadcast service to advise them on weather and farming methods, along with some light entertainment.

By later standards Doe's equipment was simple. He kept the station on the air six hours a day and used any spare time instructing farmers how to assemble radio sets. For one and a half years, he kept the station going with Mrs. Nettie Wheeler at the piano or an Edison gramaphone furnishing music between pieces of farm advice. When the company closed, Doe remained in Bellows Falls to open one of Vermont's first radio sales and repair companies.

Within a few years radio stations were in all major towns in Vermont, but it was 1954 before Vermont's first TV station, WCAX, was installed, increasing the impact of the rest of the world on a still remote and basically rural society.

103. President Calvin Coolidge — 1923 - 1928

After Plymouth's Calvin Coolidge graduated from Black River Academy and moved on to Amherst College, he continued to come home and don a homespun farmer's frock and help his father with the chores. This seemed a natural function to introverted, red-headed Calvin, the best educated man in town. He knew Greek, rhetoric, philosophy, and the classics along with the know-how of when to plant the potatoes.

When President Coolidge continued this bucolic behavior he was accused of affecting this pose for political purposes. The critics were wrong; Calvin was a farmer-scholar in the best Vermont tradition, but it was a dying breed in the 1920's.

Reading extensively about Calvin Coolidge can be a rewarding experience for Vermonters. There is much to be had on the shelves about him, for he intrigued and puzzled people who, not knowing Vermont and its people, refused to believe he was real. His *Autobiography* should convince skeptics. He was a sad man, sensitive, ornery in his own way.

Born on the Fourth of July, 1872, into an old and honorable local family, he had a sad childhood, losing his mother and sister by premature deaths. He was painfully shy, making college life a misery to him at first, but he became sufficiently social to join a fraternity and was even chosen to make the humorous class oration at graduation. After studying law with a firm in Northampton, Massachusetts, he was admitted to the Massachusetts Bar in 1897.

In 1905 Coolidge married Grace Goodhue of Burlington, a lively and pretty University of Vermont graduate who taught deaf children. Already embarked on a political career in Massachusetts, he went from one small success to larger ones, with only one defeat in his career, that of school committeeman in 1905. In 1918 he was elected Governor of Massachusetts, but he continued to live, at least on weekends, with his wife and two sons in their Northampton two-family house.

Elected Vice-President in 1920, he moved as if pre-ordained into the Presidency. When Vice-President and Mrs. Coolidge were visiting his father in Plymouth in August 1923, word came over the nearest telegraph wires that President Warren Harding had died. A few reporters and secret service men raced to Plymouth to break the news.

Many and dramatic are the accounts of what followed, but Calvin Coolidge's own laconic account in his *Autobiography* says that after his father wakened him about midnight with the news, Coolidge dressed, prayed, sent a telegram of sympathy to Mrs. Harding, and composed a public statement to reassure the people that he meant to make no sweeping changes. Then he began to look over the Constitution to see what was required in taking the oath of office.

"Having found this form in the Constitution I had it set up on the typewriter and the oath was administered by my father in his capacity as a notary public, an office he had held for a great many years. The oath was taken in what we always called the sitting room by the light of the kerosene lamp, which was the most modern form of lighting that had then reached the neighborhood."

The time was 2:47 in the morning of August 3, 1923.

In 1924 Coolidge was elected President for a full term, but four years later he did not "choose to run." He died in 1933, pre-deceased by his son Calvin.

Today visiting the Calvin Coolidge Homestead at Plymouth is a misty trip to the past, making Vermont's only elected President (Chester Arthur filled an unexpired term and was not re-elected) seem as real as a well regarded neighbor.

104. The 1927 Flood and the Great Depression of the 1930's

Practically every stream in Vermont was clogged with water wheels for sawmills, local electric power, grist mills, or power looms in 1927, before the years of community planning. When a torrential tropical storm with rain, rain, and more rain, dumped more water into the state than it could handle, Vermont experienced the biggest flood since Noah.

Mail, lights, bridges, roads, telephones, water mains, railroads, homes, factories, and barns were swept out, leaving Vermont dark, isolated, and devastated by a $30,000,000 dollar loss. This was no ordinary rampage. When the day of assessment for Vermont's worst flood came, 45 lives had been lost and no part of the state was untouched.

Much that was lost was never restored, and Vermont set out on a flood control program that changed the traditional use of waterways. No longer would streams be cluttered for local power. Flood control dams and larger power plants replaced the old mill dams and wheels. Flood control and power generation could have been combined in single dams in a more energy-conscious period.

Railroads were never fully rebuilt. Old turnpikes and town roads were replaced with highways, and Vermont's transportation changed almost completely and abruptly from horse-and-railroad to car-and-truck economy. There was a finality about the 1927 flood that old timers recall and speak of with awe, as if it closed a book on an old way of life, balanced the accounts, and began a new series.

Flood recovery was not complete by any means when the Wall Street crash reverberated in Vermont, with banks, factories, and tourist business collapsing to usher in the Great Depression. Farm prices were already low in the 1920's with overproduction and rising farm operational expenses. President Herbert Hoover's inaction caused a desperation hardly known even in the grimmest days of a century before.

But since Vermont had never been rich, being poor was not such a great fall. Despite debts, mortgages, and lack of "boughten goods" there was a tradition of can-do that enabled the people to scratch existence from the land. In fact, some of the deserted farms were taken over by refugees from the city who came to make it with only their hands for capital, just as the deserted farms of post Civil War years had been taken over by European refugees looking for a new chance.

Early 1930's newspapers report wages of $1.25 a day for 14 hours' labor in a woolen mill. When President Franklin D. Roosevelt announced his new program people read of it or listened on a rare radio with a last-ditch type of hope. Soon the Farm Credit Act aided farmers, and the Federal Emergency Relief Act and the Works Progress Administration became a part of life.

The FERA supplied clothes and canning jars in a self-help effort. The WPA not only employed people but it left its mark in better roads, town improvement, and in books, library projects, and art efforts by indigent writers and artists.

Very little has been written about Vermont and the Great Depression. It is as though it was just another of those low-key times, mercifully forgotten, only noted in the newspapers, not much worse, not much better than any other period in the ageless Green Mountains.

105. The CCC in Vermont — 1933 - 1942

When President Roosevelt announced the formation of the Civilian Conservation Corps for work in public forests in March 1933, the prospect of employment was seized by the millions of young men who were jobless, hopeless, and hungry. The general requirements were that the men be between the ages of 18 and 23, unmarried, unemployed, out of school, in good health, of good character and willing to send home about three-fourths of the approximately $30 a month pay. Interviewing boards were swamped with applicants.

Initially Vermont was allotted four camps, but a lucky variable existed here in the form of Perry Merrill, Vermont's state forester who recognized that here was a chance of a lifetime to build up Vermont's forests. Merrill's foresight had provided long range plans for conservation, flood control and forest management in the state, but lack of state funds had frustrated his efforts. Now with the Federal Government to foot the bill, Merrill was ready. Vermont had state lands crying for care.

In June 1933, the state's first CCC camp was opened at Bellows Falls with another at Mt. Tabor already authorized. Between 1933 and 1942, when war ended the program, Vermont had 24 CCC camps, although some sources give the figure as high as 39 camps. Camps opened and closed, some were authorized and not built, and some were placed on private lands. However one views it, the preponderance of CCC activity was out of all proportion to Vermont's population, to the advantage of the state.

Boys by the thousands came here from Eastern cities, again with the total number a hazy estimate depending on status, re-enlistment, and such factors. For instance, there were 5,000 older World War I veteran Bonus Army men enrolled in a few separate Vermont camps. At the outset Vermont was authorized to enroll 2,275 young men for about six months, but there were many times that number through the years.

Although established primarily for employment and conservation measures, the CCC had the stated aim of vocational training, and, depending on the camp supervisors, academic educational opportunity. Many high school equivalency certificates came from the Vermont camps, and in a few cases illiteracy was tackled with success.

Conservationist Perry Merrill reported that the work of the CCC camps put Vermont's recreational development ahead by 50 years and improved the state forests by pruning, thinning, and developing forest roads for fire protection and management purposes. They built 105 miles of road chiefly within the state forests and state parks, did pest control work on trees, flood control work, and constructed 20 miles of ski slopes, countless buildings, and miles of trails. In effect, the Vermont park system that was developed has provided the state with superior outdoor opportunities for over 40 years.

There were a few grumbles from the taxpayers that the camps were too expensive; others felt that the CCC was too oriented to the Army since every camp had a military as well as civilian director. The directorships were eagerly sought in those jobless days, and many people who took part in the program look back with nostalgia on days of living close to the soil with the sense of accomplishment in the conservation line.

At Camp Calvin Coolidge, a model for the nation, the men had a newspaper, dances, competitive sports, academic classes, a radio program, and even amateur theater. There were ski jumping, snowshoeing, summer sports, and talent nights. In Plymouth, as in all of Vermont, churches welcomed the CCC men, and though the pay was sparse the local merchants were glad to get the nickels and dimes that went toward Saturday movies and candy bars.

106. The Green Mountain Parkway — 1936

Although Vermont was staggered by the depression of the 1930's she was not for sale. The traditional integrity was as sharp as ever when the Federal Government offered the citizens a dazzling opportunity for economic prosperity in the form of a multi-million dollar national parkway to be built along the tops of the Green Mountains, cutting through rocks, forests and remote wild lands. There would be nothing like this scenic highway in the world, its promoters prophesied, but the general public looked upon it as a clearcut case of God and Mammon, judging from the letters-to-the-editors columns.

The plan was put before the legislature which voted against it, 126 to 111. Governor Charles Smith, pressured beyond belief by proponents of the parkway, called the group back into special session in the fall to reconsider, upon which the lawmakers approved the parkway but voted to send it to the people, in best Vermont tradition, to be decided by vote at Town Meetings in March 1936.

The battle raged between environmentalists and economists, capturing the national press. Vermont was to be required to put up $500,000 of the $18,000,0000 estimate, a factor in the thinking of cost-conscious taxpayers, but in retrospect it seems to have been principally a fight over whether the Green Mountains should be exploited. Bitter fighting that divided neighborhoods and families brought out record numbers of nearly 74,000 voters to the Town Meetings in which the outcome was a clear-cut rejection with 42,318 against and 30,897 in favor.

There is no evidence that this was a partisan vote, although the Democratic party was on the upswing in Vermont at that time, nor was it a rural-urban split. It appears to have been an act of conscience and deep belief. Evidently the Green Mountain Club, which had been promoting conservation in Vermont for over two decades, was important to the decision. Its members were conservative and powerful, and they used their influence to alert short-sighted opportunists to the dangers of destroying the Green Mountains.

Charles Cummings stated the position of the Green Mountain Club in the *Vermonter Magazine* as early as 1933 when the people were choosing sides for the fight. "The first thought of the average Vermonter, confronted with such a plan is, let well enough alone," he wrote. "That is what the officials of the Green Mountain Club, nearly all old men, think, even after hearing a masterly presentation of the plan in closed session, by one of the world's greatest engineers. They did not even vote on the proposition, after Col. Wilgus (backer and engineer of the plan) withdrew, because as one of them said: 'Every one of them is more opposed to it than he was before.' "

The influential old men had listened to the proposition during a thunder storm, reminiscent of the storm in which the Constitution of Vermont had been signed. Were the "Gods of the Hills" warning them, as Cummings suggests?

This story, told by vehement and vociferous proponents and opponents in the Vermont press of the 1930's parallels environmentalist-developer differences in Vermont in the 1970's.

107. World War II — 1941 - 1945

Fifty thousand Vermonters served in World War II with 1,230 killed and 3,870 wounded. A little-known fact is that Vermont declared war on Germany three months before the rest of the United States. It happened this way, according to the *New York Times* of September 16, 1941.

Early in 1941 when the National Guard was called in to Federal service, the Vermont Legislature passed a bill providing $10 a month bonus for each military person from Vermont on active duty, with the penurious stipulation that it be paid only in case of armed conflict.

Then the legislators had second thoughts about the penny pinching. When President Franklin Roosevelt gave "shooting orders" to the Navy to take any steps necessary to protect the ships in their convoys in September 1941, the Vermont Legislature by a joint resolution declared that Vermont was in "armed conflict," thus authorizing the bonus payment. Vermont and the rest of the world understood this to mean that Vermont had declared war.

The Rev. George Lansing Fox of Gilman was one of the four famed chaplains on the *USS Dorchester* who gave up their life jackets and their lives for others and went down with the ship when it was torpedoed. The four men, representing four faiths, held hands and went down singing, one of the legendary stories of the war that tug at the hearts of people.

Major-General Reginald Cram, Adjutant General of the Vermont National Guard, who saw to it that a roster of World War II military personnel was published in 1974, provided information about Vermont's part in the war.

"In keeping with Vermont tradition," he writes, "the state had the most volunteers on the basis of population of any state until sometime in 1944."

When Vermont's National Guard was called into service on February 24, 1941, there were 148 officers, one warrant, and 1,995 enlisted men in eight different units, with the vast majority in the 172nd Infantry. The Vermont National Guard first went to Camp Blanding, Florida, as part of the 43rd Division. As the armed forces expanded, replacements caused Vermont units to lose some of their local identity, but Vermont troops could be followed in campaigns, notably in New Guinea, the Solomons, and in the Philippines. One of the most famous involvements, according to General Cram, was on Rendova Island, and the Second Battalion, 172nd Infantry, received a Unit Citation for its outstanding campaign in the Ipo Dam area. After fighting in the Philippines through June 1945, a number of Vermonters went to Japan for occupation duty.

Vermont's Major-General Leonard Wing, a Rutland attorney, commanded the 86th Infantry Brigade when the National Guard was called up in 1941. He eventually became commanding general of the 43rd Infantry, one of two National Guard generals who commanded their own divisions in combat in World War II.

William H. Wills was the popular wartime governor of Vermont, serving from 1941 to 1945. When the National Guard departed, the governor was authorized to organize, equip and maintain a State Guard for local emergencies. Governor and Mrs. Wills took a parental interest in the Vermont "boys" and made trips to Camp Blanding to check on their health and morale. Prominent citizen volunteers worked with civil defense, bond sales, aid to military families, food rationing, shortages, and so on. The governor organized them into an élite "council of safety," reminding Vermonters of the people's role in warfare since the days of the New Hampshire Grants.

At the end of World War II Vermont's Senator Warren Austin, a man of broad international outlook who had helped draft the charter for the new United Nations organization, was appointed America's first delegate to the body.

108. Act 250 — 1970 - 1975

If one feature looms as the most important issue in Vermont in the third quarter of the twentieth century it is the matter of environment and development. Vermont gained attention in the nation and the world with her advanced and controversial laws to protect the land against uncontrolled development. Thoughtful observers wonder why conservative Vermont embraced the revolutionary Act 250 with its concomitant laws and rulings. Looking back 200 years there emerges a pattern of long-sighted, unselfish legislation, from the adoption of the Constitution in 1777, when the founding fathers forbade slavery in a slave society, up to the rejection of the Green Mountain Parkway in the 1930's. It has been said that Vermont Legislatures take radical measures to preserve the state's special kind of conservatism.

America was rich following World War II. Money was easy, cities were deteriorating, and people began looking for vacation homes. Vermont, not as rich as the rest of America, still had cheap lands and dilapidated farms to sell. Developmental money poured into Vermont so fast that by the mid-1960's when land rape was at its height Vermonters began to react with steely-eyed determination.

In 1969, Governor Deane Davis formed a Commission on Environmental Control to study the problems resulting from this rapid development on fragile land, sewage in streams, overworked utilities, monumental jams on country roads inadequate for metropolitan traffic, understaffed police forces, overcrowded high schools, and a rising crime rate. The prospects were for even worse conditions as the trek to the back country continued. The Commission recommended that the legislature immediately adopt a statewide set of land use planning and development regulations.

The 1970 legislature passed a basic environmental law, later referred to as Act 250, which has been blasphemed and blamed for everything from a poor hunting season to April ice storms by its opponents, but its supporters, who continue to be in the majority, have found that it works.

Here is how Act 250 operates. District Environmental Commissions appointed by the governor review applications and grant permits for major development to comply with ten criteria: will air and water be polluted?; will there be enough water for the development's use?; will there be a burden on existing water supplies?; will soil be eroded so that it cannot hold water?; can roads and other transportation handle the increased traffic?; will schools be overcrowded?; can the community provide municipal services?; will scenic beauty or wildlife and natural areas be abused?

The Act specifies that development must comply with local and regional plans. The Act also called for a Land Capability Plan, which was passed in 1973 after widespread controversy and numerous public hearings, and for a Land Use Plan. A nine member State Environmental Board acts as a court of appeals above the local commissions.

Despite rumors to the contrary Act 250 does not regulate sub-divisions of less than ten lots or residential construction of less than ten units; but it does require a permit for any structure built above 2500 feet.

By the year 2000 it can be assessed if this was indeed the great drama of this period in the history of the State of Vermont.

INDEX

U

V

W

Y

Date Due

BRODART   CAT. NO. 23 233   PRINTED IN U.S.A.